Help Me! Guide to the Nexus 5

By Charles Hughes

I0413206

Table of Contents

Getting Started

Table of Contents

1. Button Layout

The Nexus 5 has two hard buttons and three soft buttons, a microUSB port, and a headphone jack, which perform the following functions:

Figure 1: Right Side View

Power Button - Turns the phone on and off. Locks and unlocks the phone.

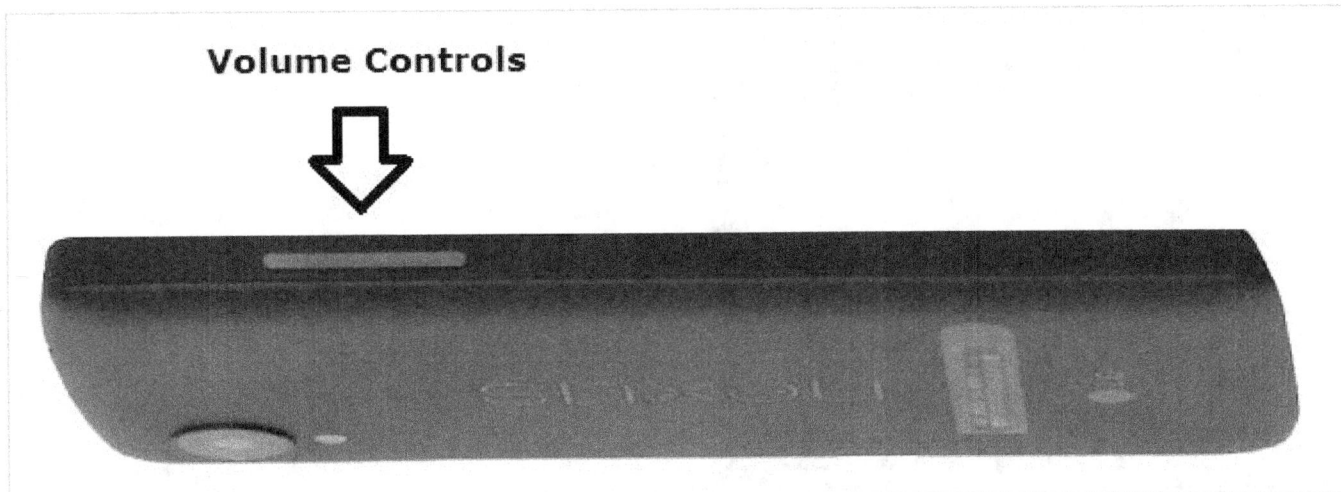

Figure 2: Left Side View

Volume Control - Controls the volume of the ear piece, speakerphone, and music.
The soft buttons only appear when the screen is turned on and the phone is unlocked. Touch a
button to perform the corresponding action:

Figure 3: Front View

Back Button - Returns the phone to the previous screen or menu.

Home Button - Returns the phone to the Home screen.

Recent Apps Button - Displays a list of all applications that were recently opened.

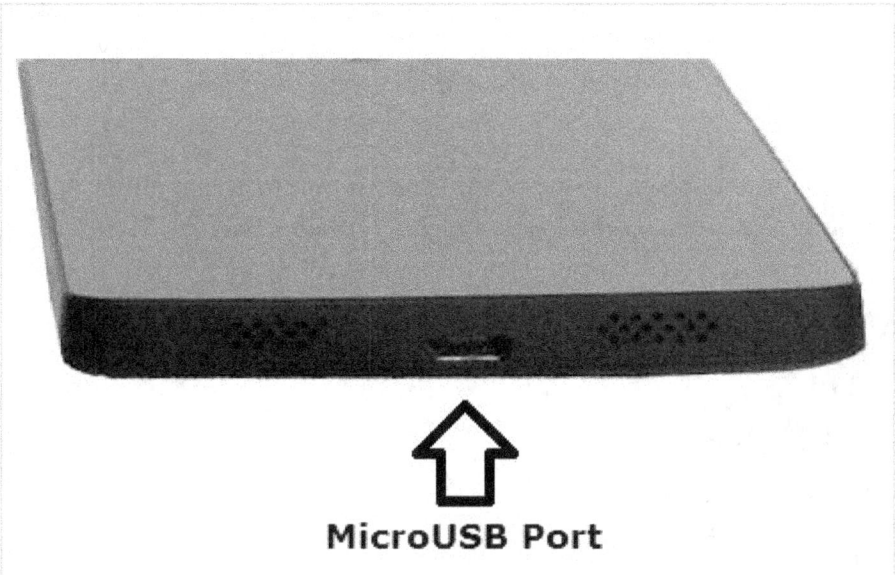

Figure 4: Bottom View

MicroUSB Port – Allows the phone to be connected to a computer in order to transfer data.

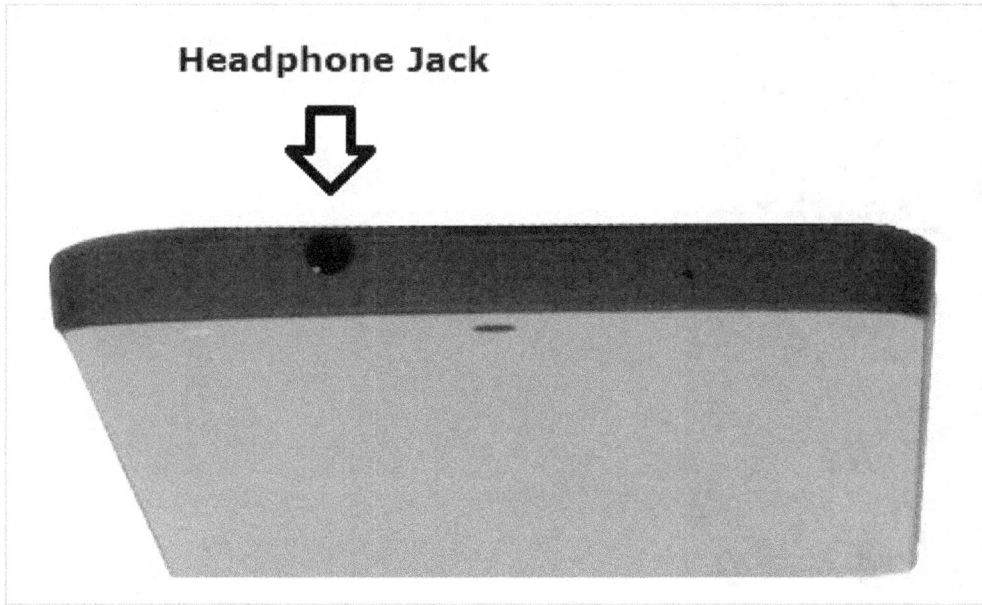

Figure 5: Top View

Headphone Jack - Allows headphones to be connected to the phone in order to listen to audio.

2. Turning the Nexus 5 On and Off

To turn the Nexus 5 on, press and hold the **Power** button for three seconds. "Google" appears and the phone starts up.

To turn the phone off, press and hold the **Power** button until the Phone Options menu appears, as shown in **Figure 6**. Touch **Power off**. A confirmation dialog appears. Touch **OK**. The Nexus 5 shuts down.

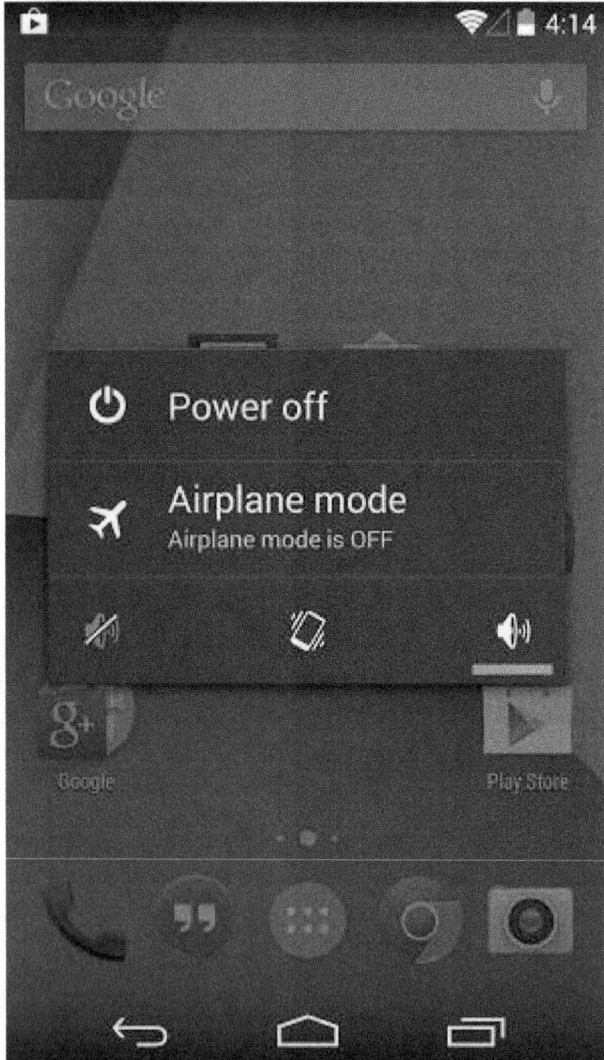

Figure 6: Phone Options Menu

3. Navigating the Screens

There are many ways to navigate the screens of the Nexus 5. Use the following tips:

- Touch the ⬠ button to return to the main Home screen at any time. Any application or tool that is currently in use will be in the same state when it is re-opened.
- Touch the ▭ button to view all recently opened applications. Touch an application to open it.
- Slide your finger to the left or right to access additional Home screens from your main Home screen.
- Touch the ⬑ button at any time to return to the previous screen, menu, or application. Once you are at the main Home screen, the ⬑ button has no function.
- Touch the top of the screen and move your finger down to view all notifications.

4. Types of Home Screen Objects

Each Home screen on the Nexus 5 is fully customizable. Refer to *"Organizing Home Screen Objects"* on page 12 to learn how to customize the Home screens. Each screen can hold one or more of the following items:

- **Widget** - A tool that can be used directly from the Home screen without having to open it first like an application. Widgets usually take up the whole screen or a fraction of it, while applications are added as icons. The Calendar widget is shown in **Figure 7**.
- **Application** - A program that opens in a new window, such as Gmail or a game. Applications are added to the Home screen as icons.
- **Folder** - A folder containing application icons. Please note that a folder cannot store widgets. Refer to *"Organizing Application Icons into Folders"* on page 121 to learn more.

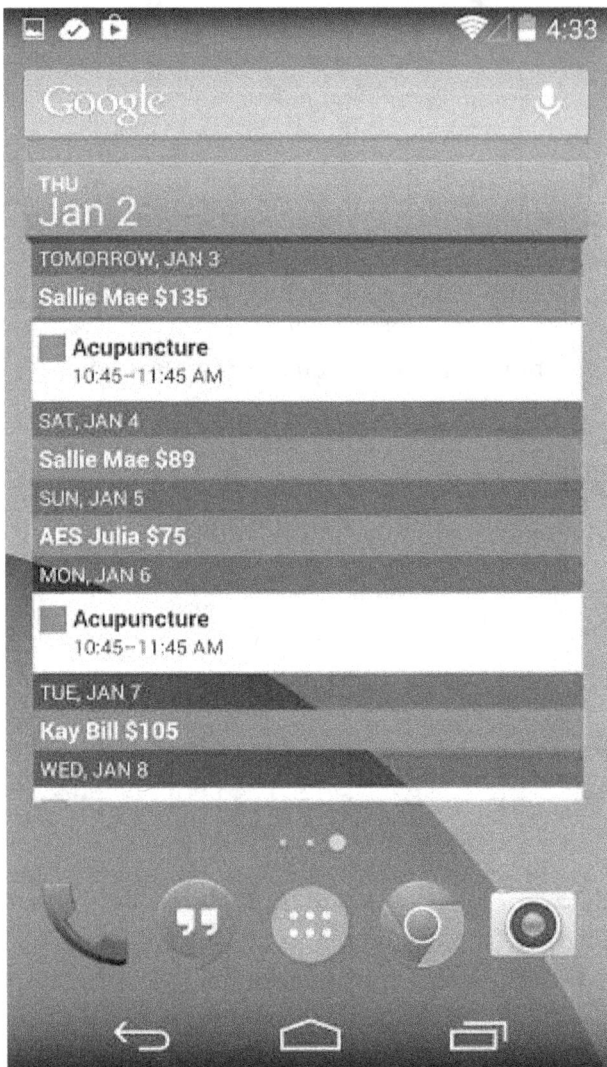

Figure 7: Calendar Widget

5. Organizing Home Screen Objects

Customize a Home screen by adding, deleting, or moving around application icons and widgets. The Nexus 5 allows you to customize five Home screens. Refer to *"Types of Home Screen Objects"* on page 11 to learn more about them.

To add an application icon or widget to a Home screen:

1. Touch the ⬤ button at the bottom of the Home screen. The Application screen appears, as shown in **Figure 8**.
2. Touch the screen and move your finger to the left or right to browse the applications and widgets that are installed on your phone.
3. Touch and hold an application or widget icon. The Home screen appears, as shown in **Figure 9**. Do not release the screen.
4. Drag the icon to the desired location. If there is no room on the current screen, drag the icon to the left or right edge of the screen. The adjacent Home screen appears.
5. Release the screen. The application icon or widget is placed.

To delete an application or widget icon from a Home screen:

1. Touch and hold an application icon or widget. The phone briefly vibrates and "Remove" appears at the top of the screen, as shown in **Figure 10**. Do not release the screen.
2. Drag the icon to the top of the screen. The object turns red.
3. Release the screen. The application icon or widget is deleted from the Home screen.

Note: To move an object to another location on the Home screen, touch and hold the object until the phone briefly vibrates and "Remove" appears at the top of the screen. Move the object to the desired location and release the screen. The object is placed in the new location. You cannot place an object on a page that is full or on top of another object, unless it is a folder.

Figure 8: Application Screen

Figure 9: Home Screen while Adding Objects

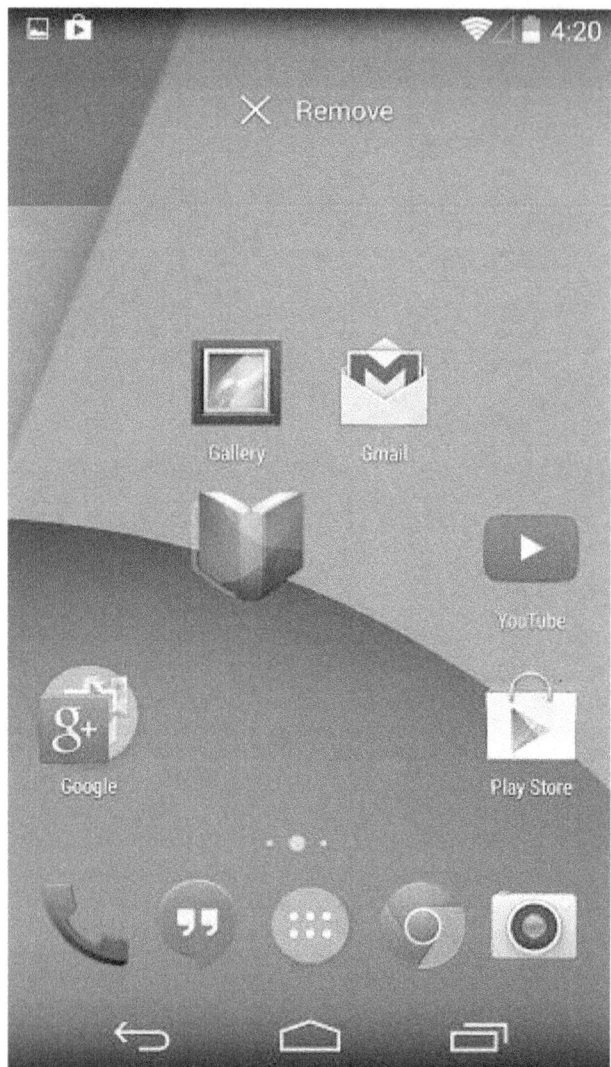

Figure 10: Home Screen while Moving Icons

6. Transferring Files to the Nexus 5 Using a PC or Mac

Media files that you have obtained elsewhere can be imported to the Nexus 5. To import media:

1. Connect the Nexus 5 to your PC or Mac using the provided USB cable. "Connected as a media device" appears in the status bar. The PC automatically recognizes the Nexus 5, but the Mac needs an additional application in order to transfer files to the phone. If you are using a Mac, download the Android File Transfer application at **www.android.com/filetransfer/** before proceeding.
2. Open the **Computer** folder on a PC (or **My Computer** on Windows XP or older) and double-click the 'Nexus 5' portable device. On a Mac, open the Android File Transfer program. The Nexus 5 folder opens.
3. Double-click the **Internal Storage** folder, if you are using a PC. The Nexus 5 Folders appear on a PC, as shown in **Figure 11**, or on a Mac, as shown in **Figure 12**.
4. Double-click a folder. The folder opens.
5. Drag and drop a file into the open folder. The file is copied and will appear in the corresponding library.

Note: When copying eBooks to the Nexus 5, drag and drop the files into the corresponding folder. For instance, eBooks you wish to read using the Kindle Reader for Android should be copied to the 'kindle' folder.

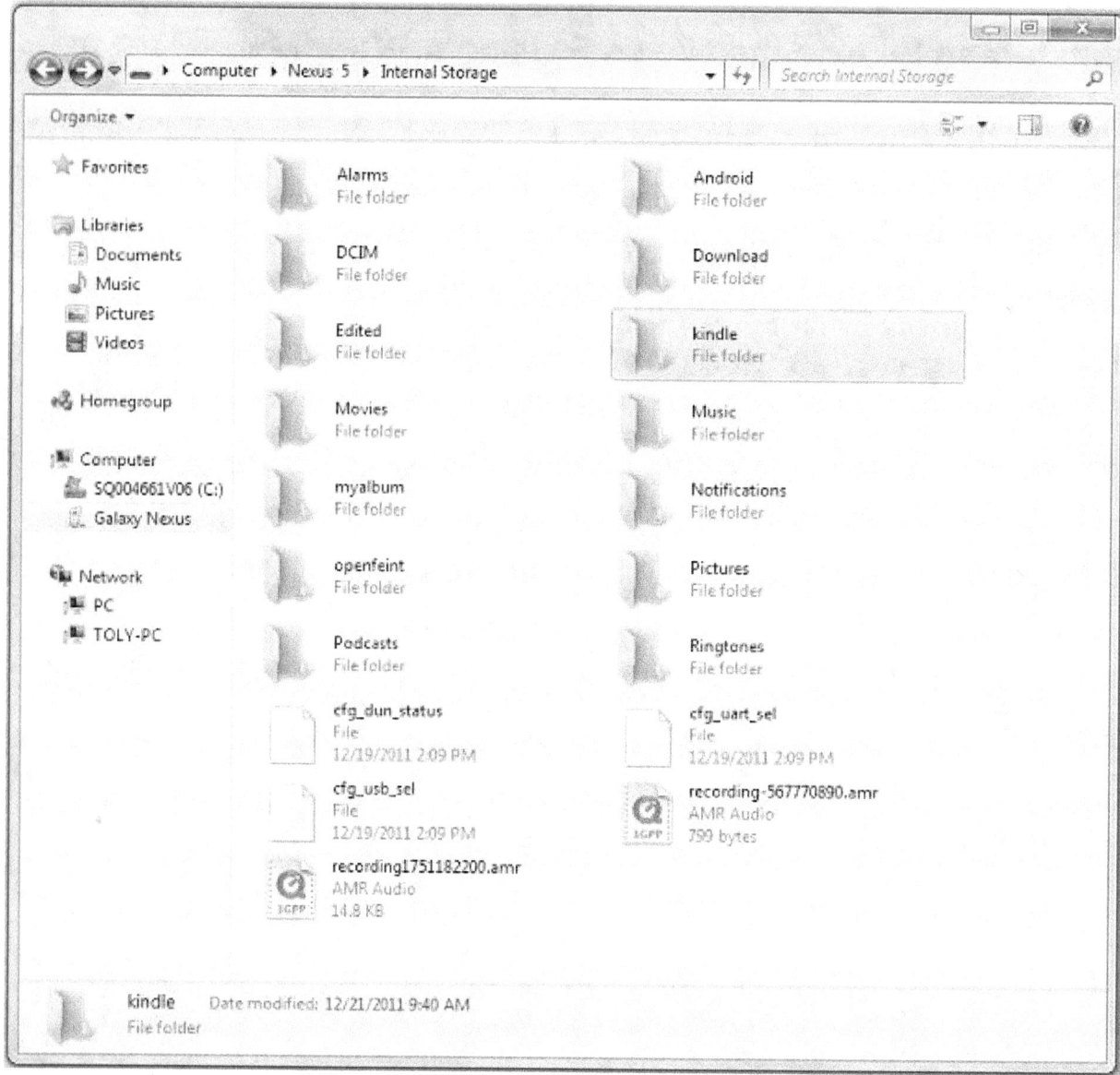

Figure 11: Nexus 5 Folders on a PC

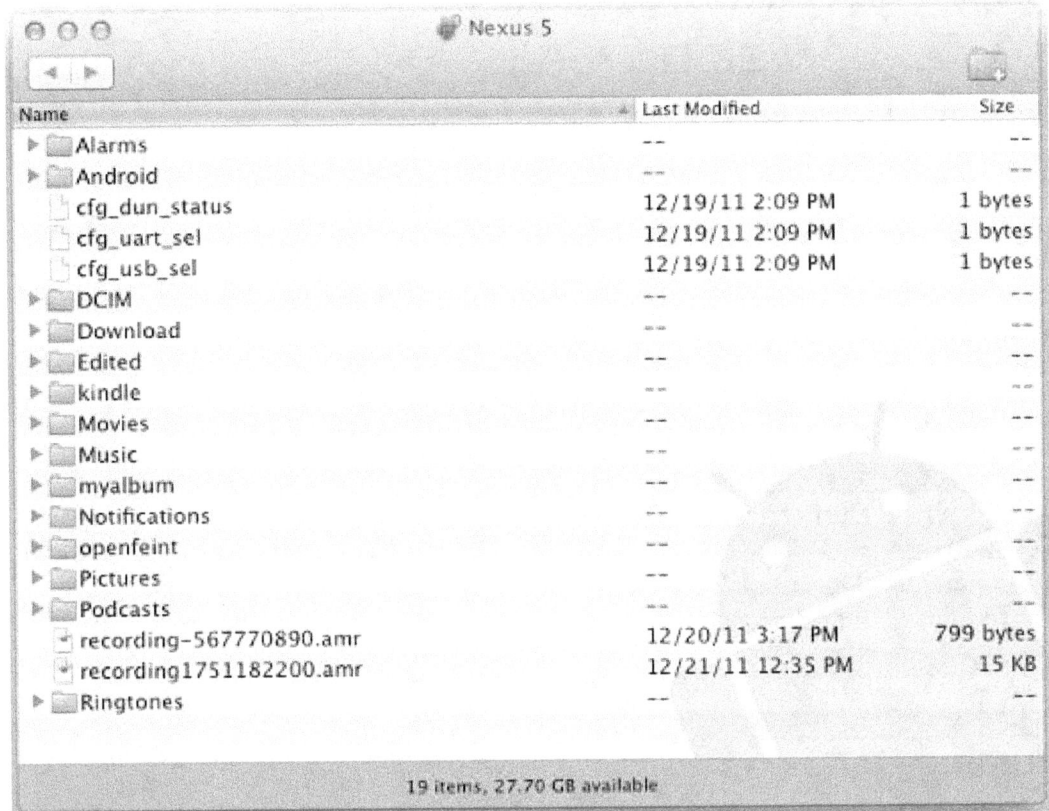

Figure 12: Nexus 5 Folders on a Mac

Making Calls

Table of Contents

1. Dialing a Number

Numbers that are not in your phonebook can be dialed on the keypad. To manually dial a phone number, touch the 📞 icon at the bottom of the screen. The keypad appears, as shown in **Figure 1**. If you do not see the keypad, touch the ⚏ icon at the bottom of the screen. Enter a phone number and touch the 📞 button at the bottom of the screen. The phone calls the number.

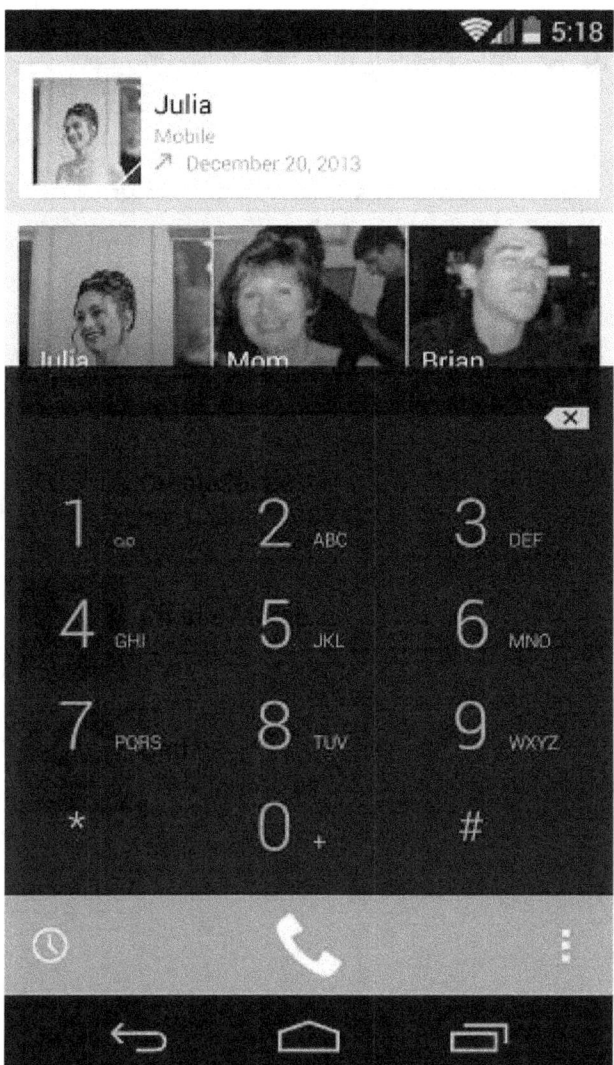

Figure 1: Phone Keypad

2. Calling a Contact

If a number is stored in your phonebook, you may touch the name of a contact to dial it. Refer to *"Adding a New Contact"* on page 32 to learn how to add a contact to the phonebook. To call a contact already stored in your Phonebook:

1. Touch the ![icon] icon at the bottom of the Home screen, or touch the ![icon] icon and then touch the ![icon] icon from the application list. The Phonebook appears, as shown in **Figure 2**.
2. Touch a contact's name. The Contact Information screen appears, as shown in **Figure 3**.
3. Touch the number that you wish to call. The Nexus 5 dials the number.

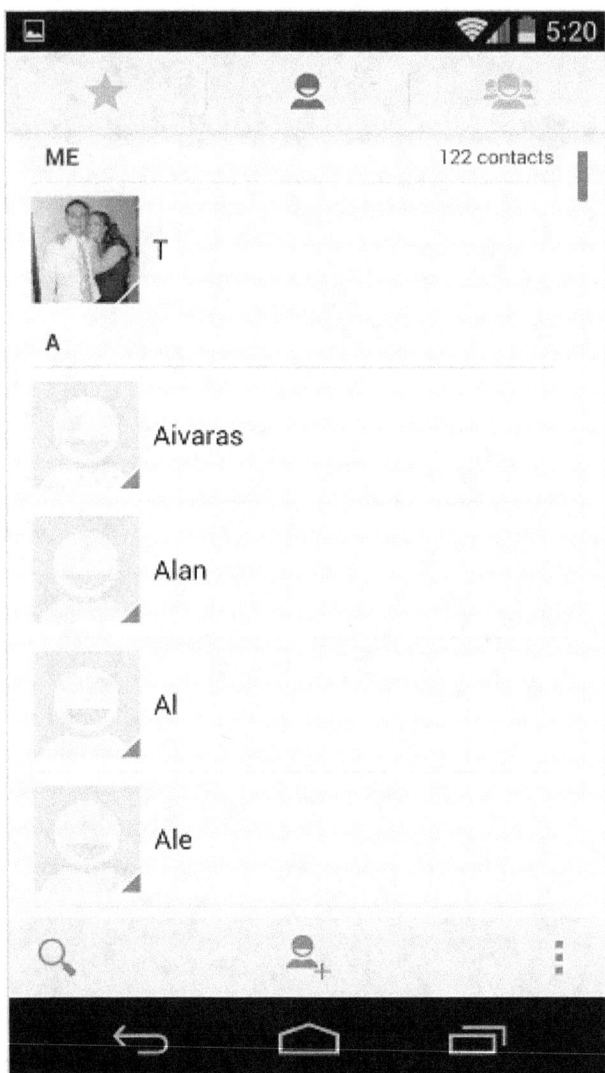

Figure 2: Phonebook

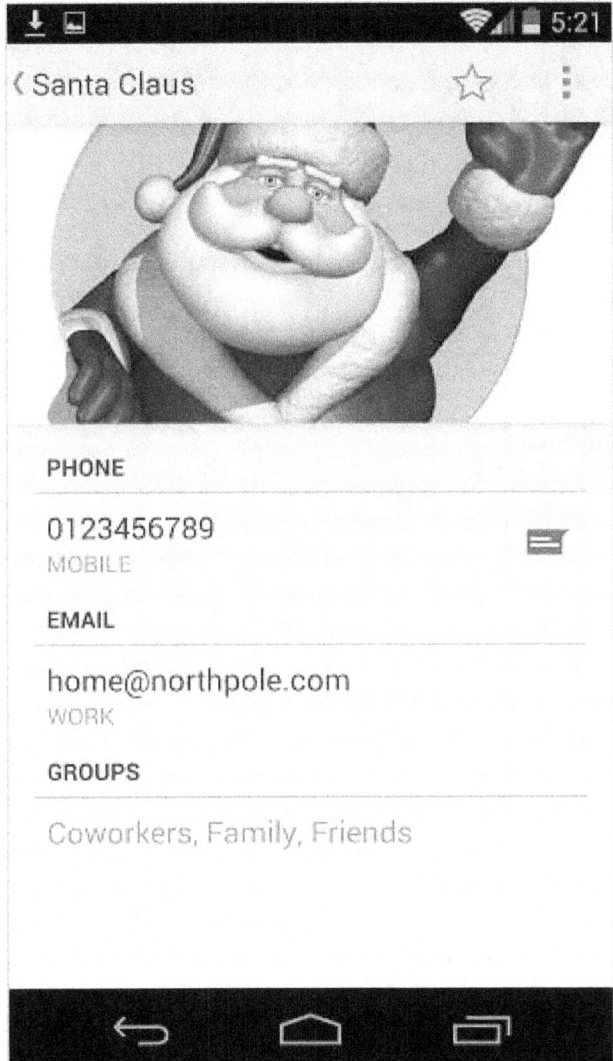

Figure 3: Contact Information Screen

3. Calling a Frequently Dialed Number

You can add a Direct Dial shortcut to the Home screen, which immediately dials a number stored in your phonebook when you touch it. To add and use a Direct Dial shortcut:

1. Touch and hold an empty spot on a Home screen. The Home screen menu appears, as shown in **Figure 4**.
2. Touch the ▦ icon at the bottom of the screen. The Widgets screen appears, as shown in **Figure 5**.
3. Touch the screen and move your finger to the left. Additional widgets appear.
4. Touch and hold the 😊 icon. The Home screen appears. Do not release the screen.
5. Drag the 😊 icon to the desired location and release the screen. The 😊 icon is placed and your phonebook appears.
6. Touch a phone number. The Direct Dial shortcut is set and the icon appears on the Home screen. The contact's photo appears in place of the icon, if one has been assigned to the contact.
7. Touch the **Direct Dial** icon. The number is dialed.

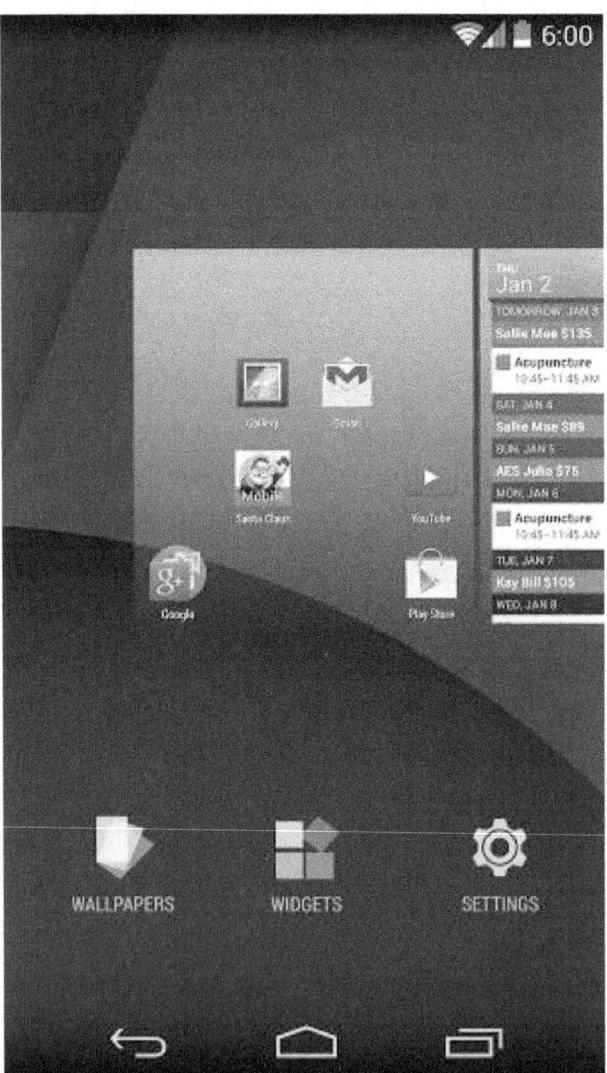

Figure 4: Home Screen Menu

Figure 5: Widgets Screen

4. Returning a Recent Phone Call

After you miss a call, the Nexus 5 will notify you of who called and at what time. The phone also shows a history of all recent calls. To view and return a missed call or redial a recently entered number:

1. Touch the ![phone icon] icon at the bottom of the screen. The keypad appears.

2. Touch the ![clock icon] icon at the top of the screen. A full list of recent calls appears, as shown in **Figure 6**. Touch the screen anywhere, and move your finger to the left to view only the recently missed calls.

3. Touch the ![phone button] button next to a number. The number is dialed.

Figure 6: Full List of Recent Calls

5. Receiving a Voice Call

When receiving a voice call, the Incoming Call screen appears, as shown in **Figure 7**. To answer the call, touch the ☎ icon and move your finger to the right until it is over the ☎ icon. The call is connected. To decline the call, touch the ☎ icon and move your finger to the left until it is over the ☎ icon. The call is sent to voicemail.

Figure 7: Incoming Call Screen

6. Using the Speakerphone During a Voice Call

The Nexus 5 has a built-in Speakerphone, which is useful when calling from a car or when several people need to participate in a conversation. To use the Speakerphone during a phone call:

1. Place a phone call. The Calling Screen appears, as shown in **Figure 8**.

2. Touch the icon at the bottom of the screen. The speakerphone turns on.

3. Adjust the volume of the Speakerphone using the Volume Controls. Refer to *"Button Layout"* on page 6 to locate the Volume Controls.

4. Touch the icon. The speakerphone turns off.

Figure 8: Calling Screen

7. Using the Keypad During a Voice Call

You may wish to use the keypad while on a call in order to input numbers in an automated menu or to enter an account number. To use the keypad during a voice call, place the call and touch

the ⊞ icon at the bottom left corner of the screen. The keypad appears, as shown in **Figure 9**. To

hide the keypad, touch the ⊞ icon.

Figure 9: Phone Keypad While on a Call

8. Using the Mute Function During a Voice Call

During a voice call, you may wish to mute your side of the conversation. When mute is turned on, the person on the other end of the line will not hear anything on your side. To use Mute during a call, place a voice call and touch the 🎤 icon at the bottom of the screen. The phone mutes your voice and the caller(s) can no longer hear you, but you are still able to hear them. Touch the 🎤 icon again. Mute is turned off.

9. Starting a Conference Call (Adding a Call)

To talk to more than one person at a time, place a new call without ending the current one. To add a call:

1. Make a call. The call is connected and the Calling screen appears.

2. Touch the 👤 icon at the bottom of the screen. The keypad appears.

3. Dial a number and touch the 📞 button at the bottom of the screen. The phone dials the second number.

4. Touch the 🧍 button once connected. The calls are merged and a three-person conference call is started, as shown in **Figure 10**.

Figure 10: Conference Call

Managing Contacts

Table of Contents

1. Adding a New Contact

The Nexus 5 can store phone numbers, email addresses, and other contact information in its phonebook. To add a new contact to the phonebook:

1. Touch the icon at the bottom of the Home screen, or touch the icon and then touch the icon from the application list. The Phonebook appears, as shown in **Figure 1**.

2. Touch the icon at the bottom of the screen. The Account confirmation dialog appears, which asks you whether you wish to add the contact under the current account, allowing you to view the contact on every device registered to the same account.

3. Touch **OK** to add the contact under the current account or touch **Add new account** to add the contact to a different account. After touching 'OK' or adding a new account, the New Contact screen appears, as shown in **Figure 2**. Refer to *"Adding a Google Account to the Phone"* on page 91 to learn more.

4. Touch each field to edit it. Enter the contact's information in each field.

5. Touch **Done** in the upper left-hand corner of the screen when you are finished. The contact's information is stored in the phonebook.

Note: To hide the keyboard at any moment, touch the *key at the bottom of the screen. Refer to* "Tips and Tricks" *on page 174 to learn more about adding a new contact, including a tip on adding an extension to a phone number.*

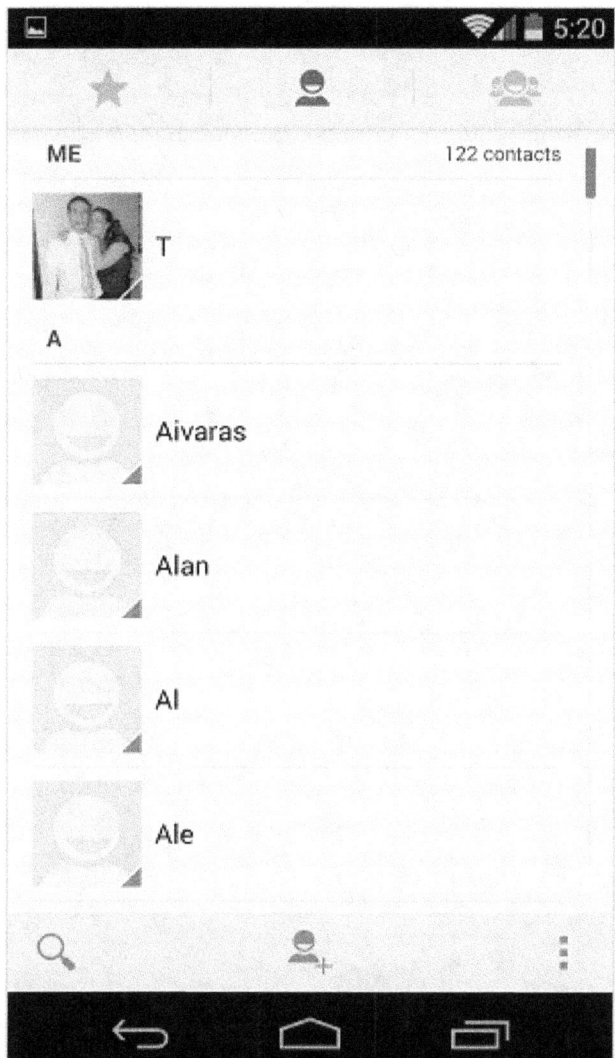

Figure 1: Phonebook

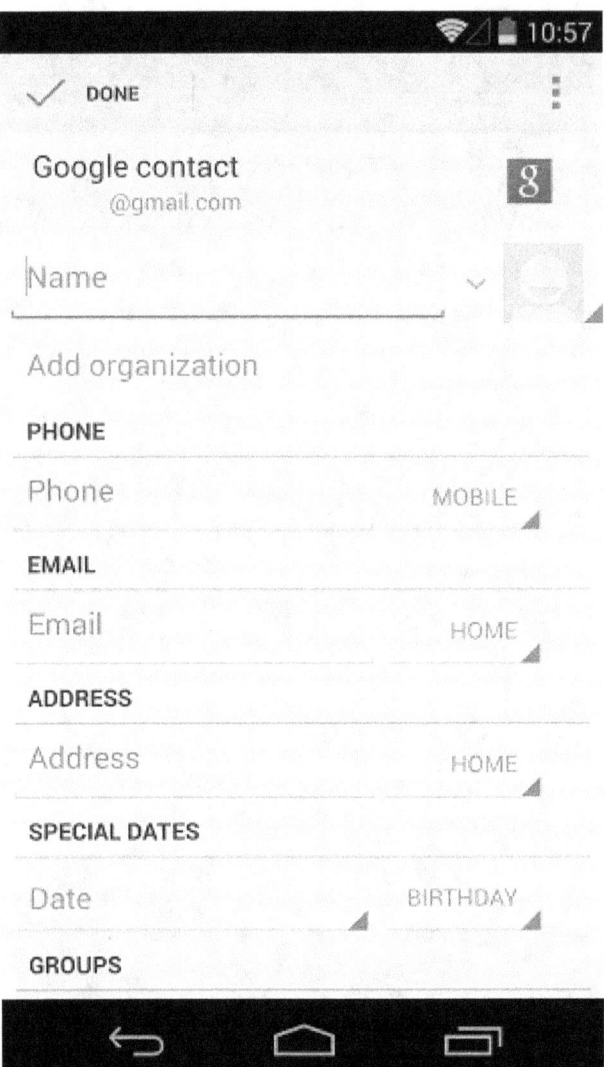

Figure 2: New Contact Screen

2. Finding a Contact

After adding a contact to your phonebook, you may search for it. To find a stored contact:

1. Touch the [icon] icon at the bottom of the Home screen or touch the [icon] icon and then touch the [icon] icon from the application list. The phonebook appears.
2. Touch the [icon] button. The search field appears.
3. Start typing the name of the contact. The phone searches as you type and the possible contact matches appear, as shown in **Figure 3**.

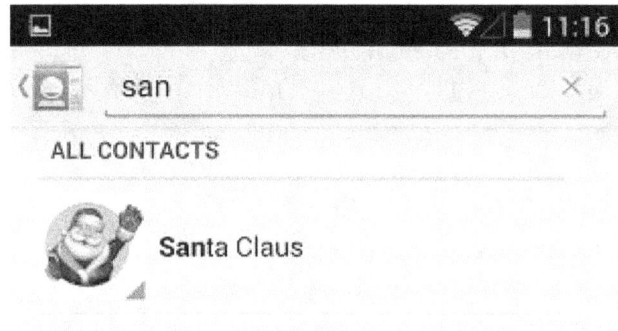

Figure 3: Possible Contact Matches

3. Editing Contact Information

After adding contacts to the phonebook, you may edit them at any time. To edit an existing contact's information:

1. Touch the ⬛ icon or touch the ● icon and then touch the ⬛ icon from the application list. The phonebook appears.
2. Touch the contact's name. The Contact Information screen appears, as shown in **Figure 4**.
3. Touch the ⫶ icon in the upper right-hand corner of the screen. The Contact menu appears, as shown in **Figure 5**.
4. Touch **Edit**. The Contact Editing screen appears.
5. Touch a field to edit it. Enter the contact's information into each field.
6. Touch **Done** in the upper left-hand corner of the screen. The contact's information is updated.

Note: To hide the keyboard at any time, touch the ⌄ *key at the bottom of the screen.*

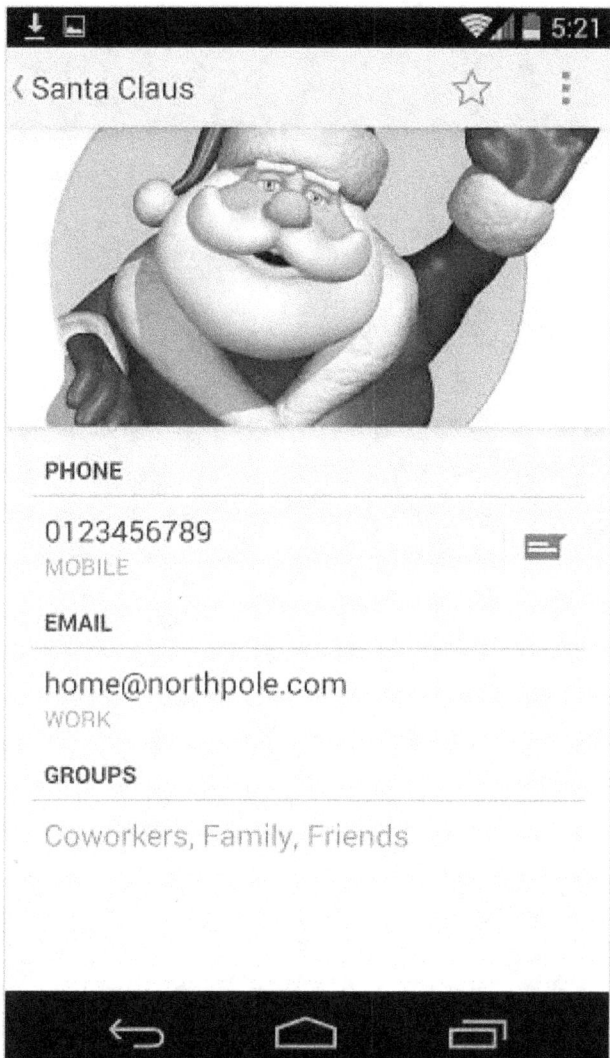

Figure 4: Contact Information Screen

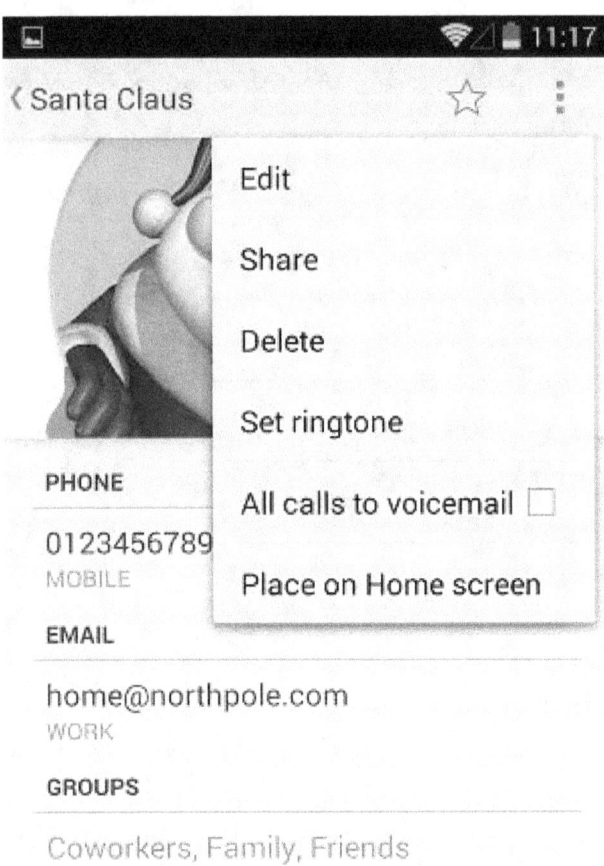

Figure 5: Contact Menu

4. Deleting a Contact

You may delete a contact from the phonebook in order to free up space or for organizational purposes. To delete an unwanted contact:

1. Touch the icon or touch the icon and then touch the icon from the application list. The phonebook appears.
2. Touch the contact's name. The Contact Information screen appears.
3. Touch the icon in the upper right-hand corner of the screen. The Contact menu appears.

4. Touch **Delete**. A confirmation dialog appears.
5. Touch **OK**. The contact is deleted.

5. Assigning a Photo to a Contact

You can assign a personal photo to a contact, which will appear next to the contact's name in the phonebook and when the contact calls. An existing photo can be assigned from the Gallery or a picture may be taken and assigned.

To assign a photo from the Gallery to a contact:

1. Touch the icon or touch the icon and then touch the icon from the application list. The phonebook appears.
2. Touch the contact's name. The Contact Information screen appears.
3. Touch the icon at the top of the screen (just below the contact's name). The Assign Photo menu appears, as shown in **Figure 6**.
4. Touch **Choose photo from Gallery**. The Gallery opens.
5. Touch an album. The album opens.
6. Touch a photo thumbnail. The Crop screen appears, as shown in **Figure 7**.
7. Touch the icons in the corners of the picture, and drag them in any direction to resize the crop. Touch the center of the photo and drag your finger to select the desired section of the photo.
8. Touch **OK** in the upper right-hand corner of the screen. The photo is assigned to the contact.

To take a picture and assign it to a contact:

1. Follow steps 1-5 above. The Assign Photo menu appears.
2. Touch **Take photo**. The camera turns on, as shown in **Figure 8**. Touch the icon if you wish to switch between the front and rear cameras.
3. Touch the button at the bottom of the screen. The camera takes a picture and a preview of it appears.

4. Touch the ✔ button in the bottom right-hand corner of the screen. The Crop screen appears. If you wish to retake the picture instead, touch the ↻ icon while previewing the photo. You can also touch the ✕ icon while previewing the photo to return to the Assign Photo menu without saving the captured image.

5. Touch the ○ icons and drag them in any direction to resize the crop. Touch the center of the photo and drag your finger to select the correct section of the photo. Touch **OK** in the upper right-hand corner of the screen. The photo is assigned to the contact.

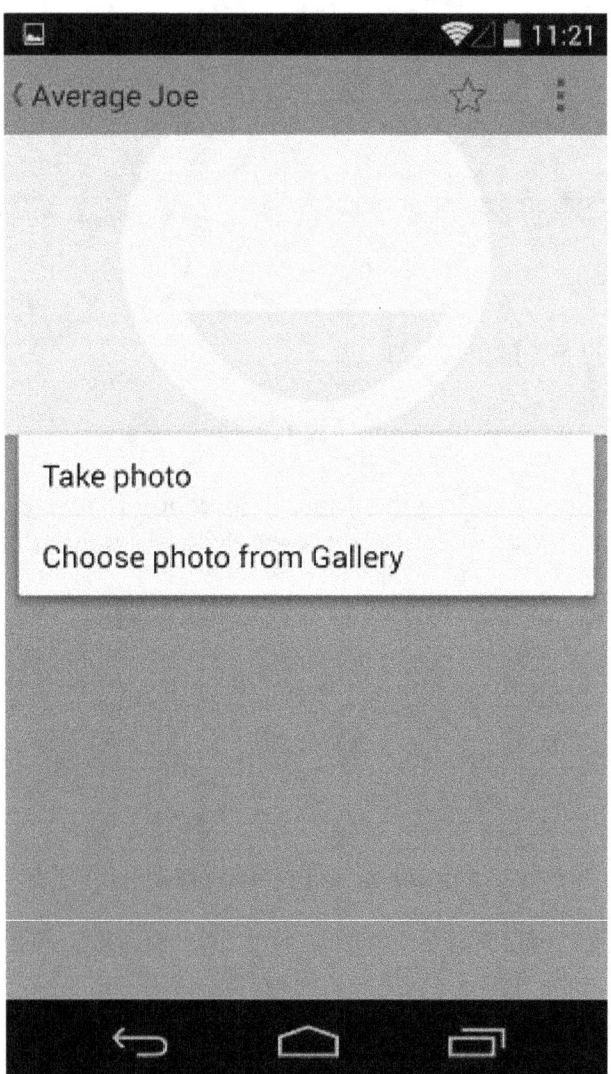

Figure 6: Assign Photo Menu

Figure 7: Crop Screen

Figure 8: Camera Turned On

6. Sharing a Contact's Information

When a contact is stored in the phonebook, all of the information for that contact can be shared. To share a contact's information with someone else:

1. Touch the ☺ icon. The phonebook appears.
2. Touch the contact's name. The Contact Information screen appears.

3. Touch the ⋮ icon in the upper right-hand corner of the screen. The Contact menu appears.
4. Touch **Share**. The Sharing Method menu appears, as shown in **Figure 9**.

5. Touch **Gmail**. The New Email screen appears with the contact's information attached, as shown in **Figure 10**.
6. Enter the recipient's email address. The email address is entered.
7. Touch the **Subject** and **Compose email** fields to enter a topic for the email and a message, respectively.
8. Touch the ➤ button in the upper right-hand corner of the screen. The contact's information is sent to the selected recipient.

Note: Sending contact information via Bluetooth is possible but is only for advanced users, and is not discussed in this basic guide.

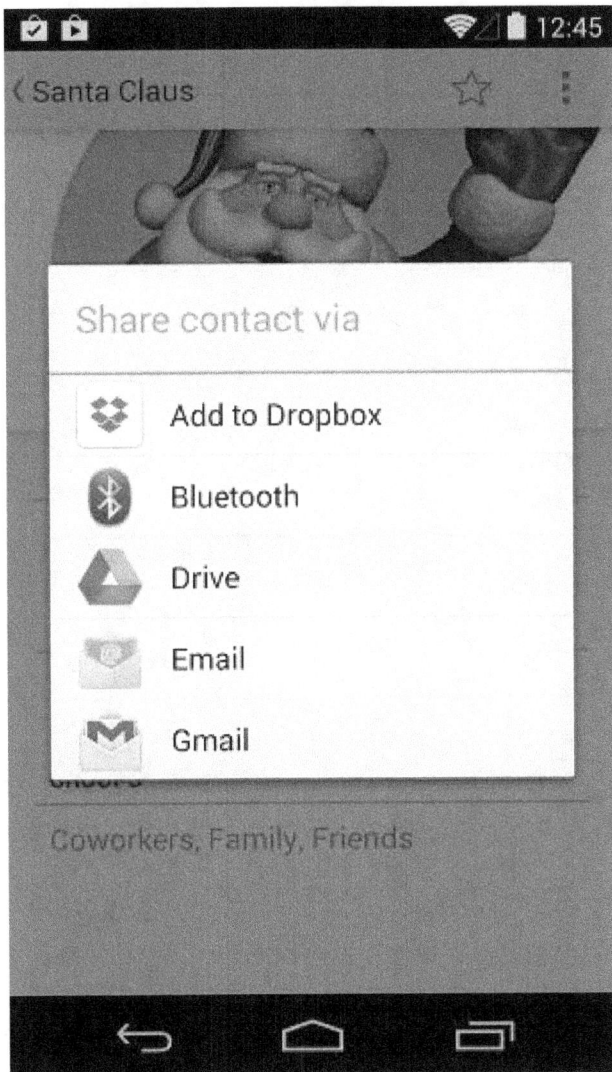

Figure 9: Sharing Method Menu

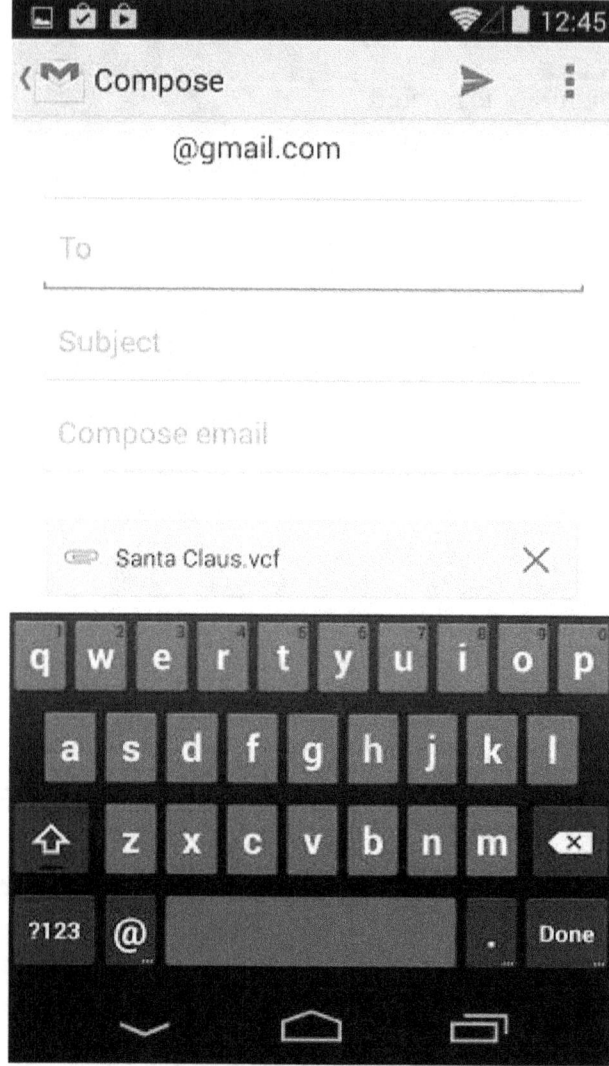

Figure 10: New Email Screen

7. Backing Up Contacts

There is no need to manually back up contacts on your Nexus 5. When you log in to a Google account, the contacts are automatically backed up on Google's servers and made accessible from any device registered under the same account. If you do not have a Google account, please register at **https://accounts.google.com/signup**.

Text Messaging

Table of Contents

1. Composing a New Text Message

The Nexus 5 can send text messages to other mobile phones. On the Nexus 5, the messaging application and Google Talk have been combined into one application, called Hangouts. Do not worry, as it is still very easy to send a simple text message. To compose a new text message:

1. Touch the icon at the bottom of the Home screen. The Hangouts application opens, as shown in **Figure 1**.

2. Touch the icon in the upper right-hand corner of the screen. The New Hangout screen appears, as shown in **Figure 2**. Suggested contacts are listed on this screen.

3. Touch the name of a contact on this screen, or touch the empty field at the top of the screen and enter a phone number. Suggestions appear while typing. Touch the name of a contact at any time to select him or her. The New Text Message screen appears, as shown in **Figure 3**.

4. Enter a message and touch the button. The message is sent and appears as a conversation, sorted by send date, as shown in **Figure 4**.

Figure 1: Hangouts Application

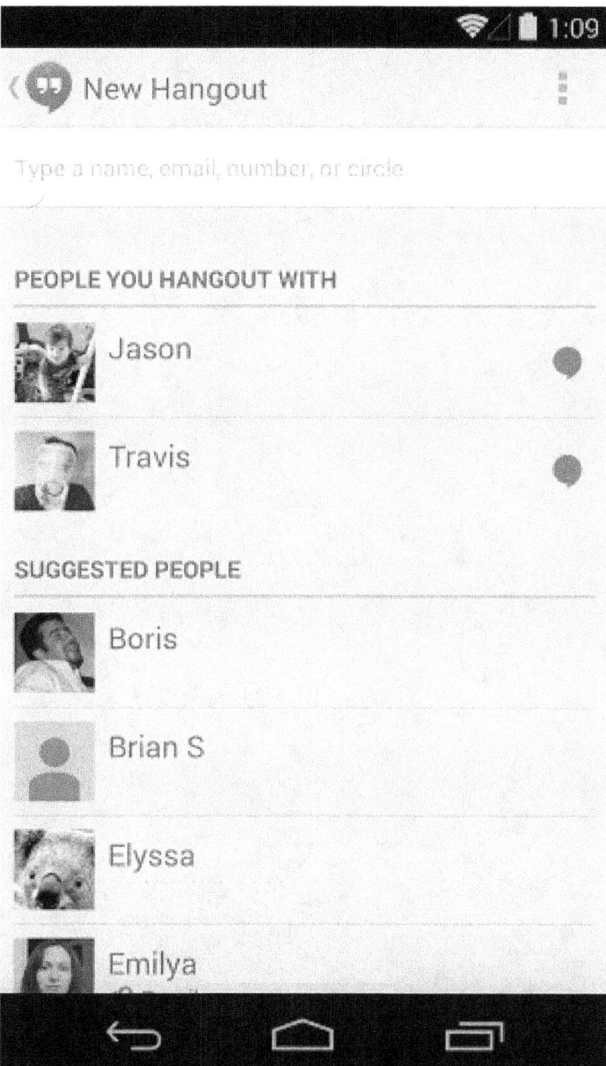

Figure 2: New Hangout Screen

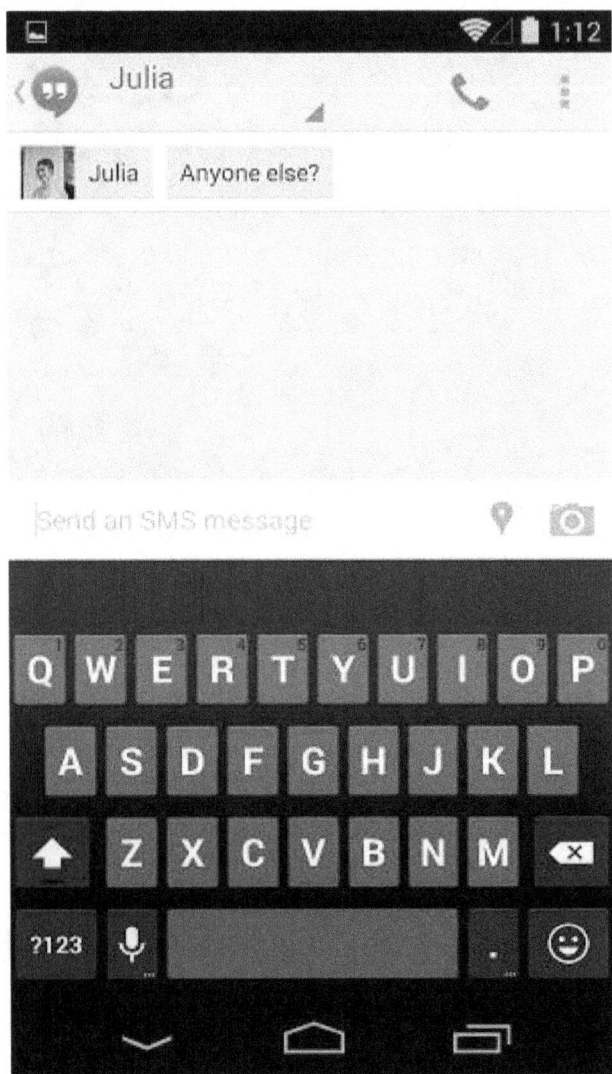

Figure 3: New Text Message Screen

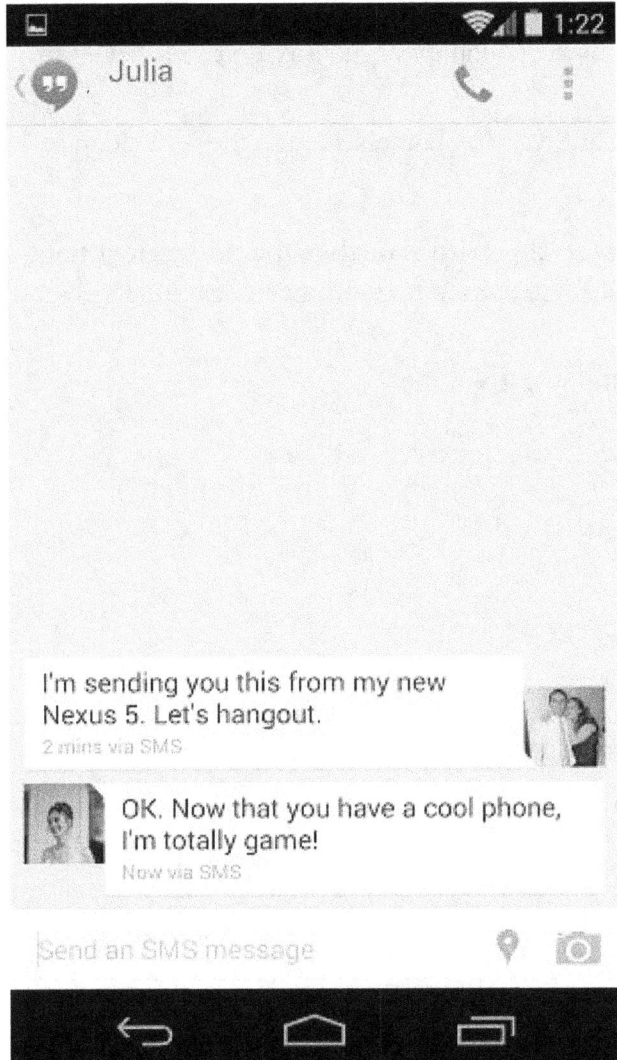

Figure 4: Text Message Conversation

2. Copying, Cutting, and Pasting Text

The Nexus 5 allows you to copy or cut text from one location and paste it to another. Copying leaves the text in its current location and allows you to paste it elsewhere. Cutting deletes the text from its current location and allows you to paste it elsewhere. To cut, copy, and paste text:

1. Touch and hold text on the screen. The text options appear, as outlined in **Figure 5**. To learn how to compose a message, refer to *"Composing a New Text Message"* on page 44.
2. Touch one of the following icons at the top of the screen to perform the associated action:

- Selects all of the text in the field.

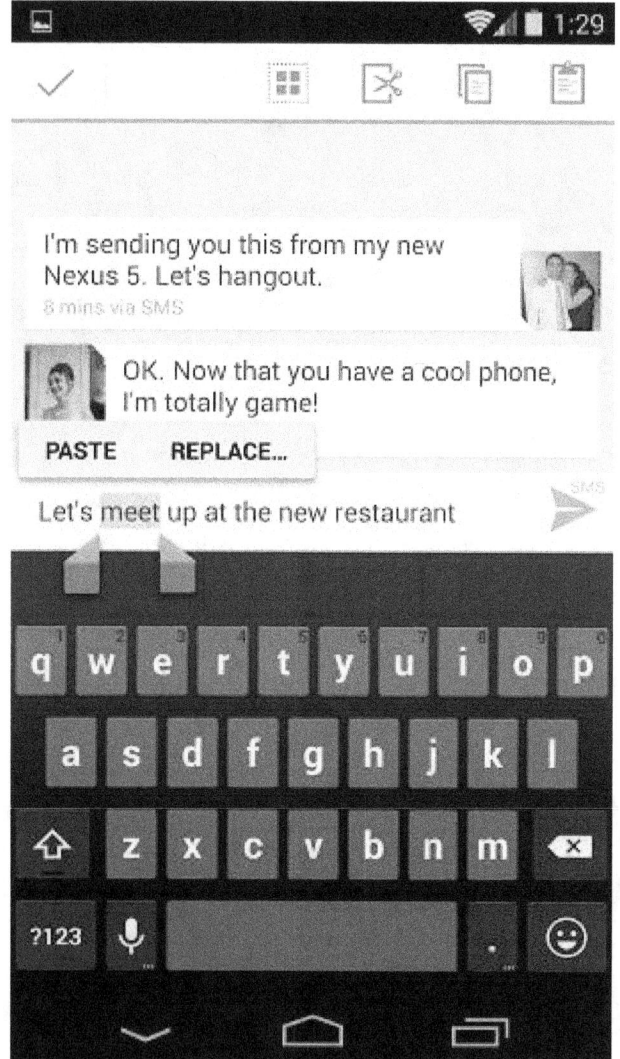 - Removes the text while copying it to the clipboard. Touch and hold any text field, even in

an outside application, and touch **Paste** to enter the cut text. You can also touch the icon at the top of the screen to paste text.

- Leaves the text in the field while copying it to the clipboard. Touch and hold any text field, even in an outside application, and touch **Paste** to enter the copied text. You can also touch

the icon at the top of the screen to paste text into the current message.

Note: The 'cut' and 'copy' options only become available when text is selected.

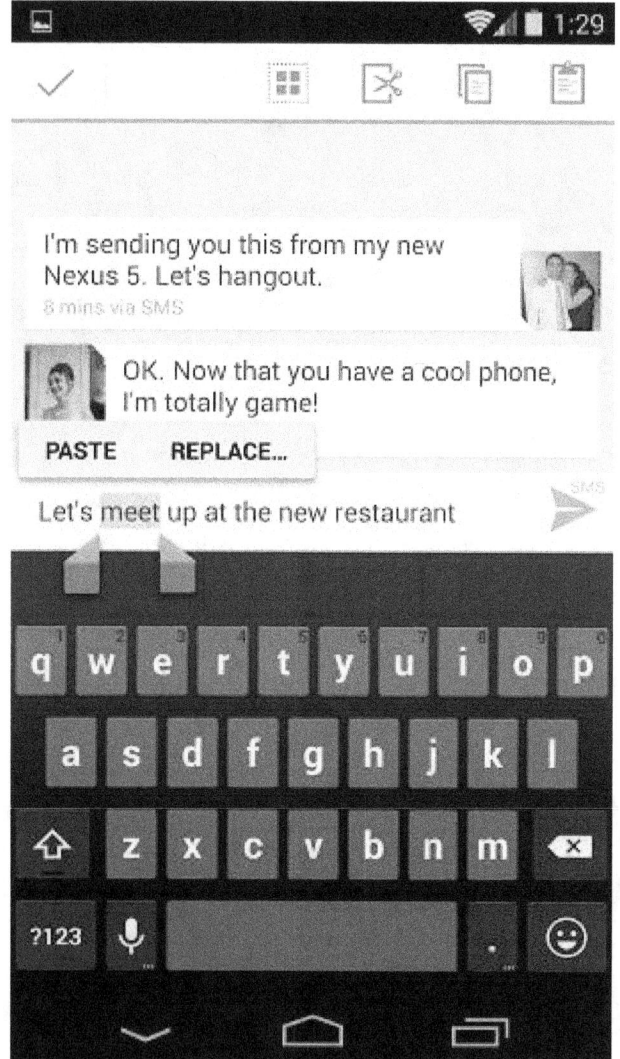

Figure 5: Text Options

3. Using the Auto-Complete Feature

While entering a text message, the Nexus 5 automatically makes suggestions to auto-complete words, which appear above the virtual keyboard, as outlined in **Figure 6**. This is especially useful when a word is very long. To accept a suggestion, touch the word. The word is inserted into the current message.

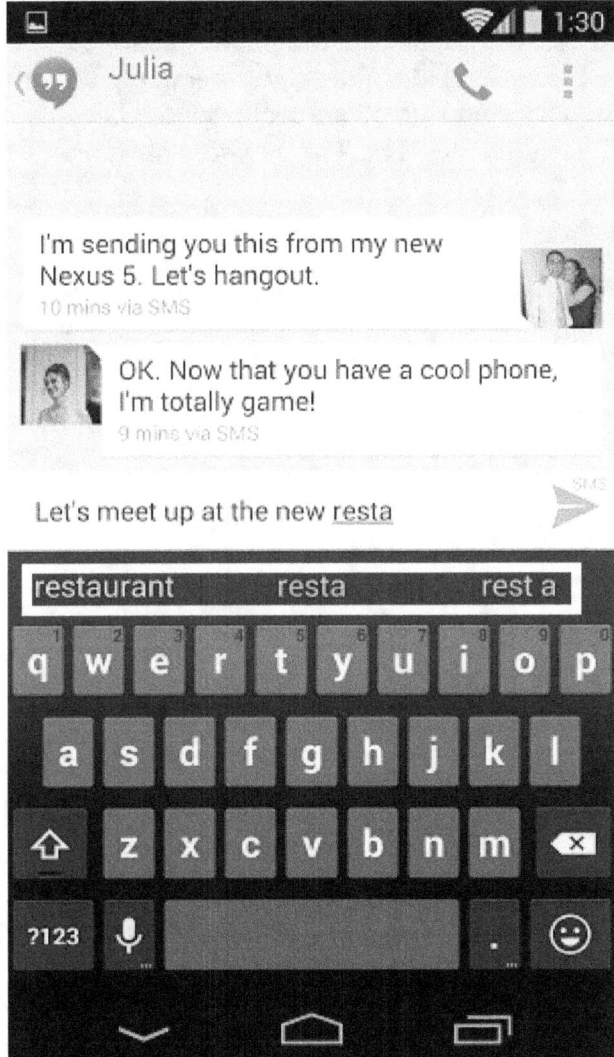

Figure 6: Auto Suggestions

4. Receiving Text Messages

The phone can receive text messages from any other mobile phone, including non-smartphones. When receiving a text, the phone vibrates once, plays a sound, or both, depending on the settings. Refer to *"Setting the Ringtone, Media, and Alarm Volume"* on page 142 to learn how to set text message notifications.

A new text message does not automatically pop up on the screen. Instead, the icon appears at the top left of the screen. To open a newly received text message, touch the status bar at the top of the screen and drag it down (the bar where the time, battery, and signal bars are located). The Notifications screen appears, as shown in **Figure 7**. Touch the message. The new text message opens.

Figure 7: Notifications Screen

5. Reading Text Messages

You may read any text message that you have received, provided that you have not deleted it. To read stored text messages, touch the [icon] icon. The Hangouts application opens. Touch a conversation. The conversation opens.

6. Forwarding Text Messages

The forwarding feature on the phone allows a text message to be copied in full and sent to other recipients. To forward a text message:

1. Touch the [icon] icon. The Hangouts application opens.
2. Touch a conversation. The conversation opens.
3. Touch and hold a text message. The Message options appear, as shown in **Figure 8**.
4. Touch **Forward**. A list of available hangouts appears.
5. Touch the name of a contact. The corresponding conversation appears with the forwarded message copied into the text field. You may also touch **New Hangout** at the bottom of the screen to start a new conversation. Once you have started the new conversation, the message will be automatically copied into the text field.

6. Touch the [icon] button. The text message is forwarded.

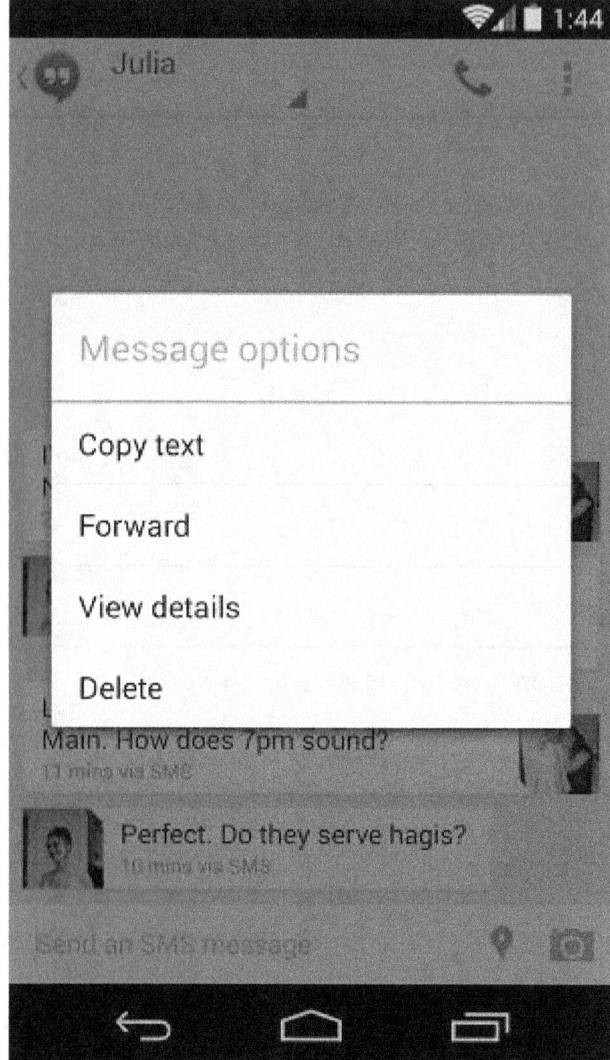

Figure 8: Message Options

7. Calling the Sender from within a Text

After receiving a text message from a contact, you may call that person without exiting the text message. To call someone from whom you have received a text message:

1. Touch the 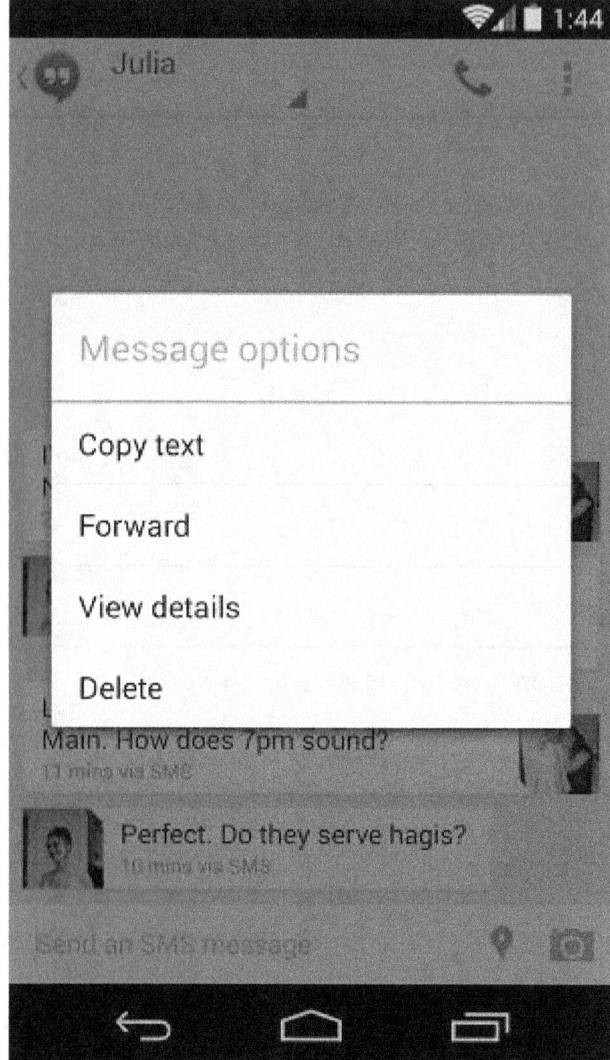 icon. The Hangouts application opens.
2. Touch a conversation. The Conversation opens.

3. Touch the button at the top of the screen. The number is dialed.

8. Deleting Text Messages

The Nexus 5 can delete separate text messages or an entire conversation, which is a series of text messages between you and a single contact.

Warning: Once deleted, text messages cannot be restored.

To delete an entire conversation:

1. Touch the icon. The Hangouts application opens.
2. Touch and hold a conversation. "Select conversations" appears at the top of the screen.
3. Touch the icon in the upper right-hand corner the screen. A confirmation dialog appears.
4. Touch **Delete**. The conversation is deleted.

To delete a separate text message:

1. Touch the icon. The Hangouts application opens.
2. Touch a conversation. The conversation opens.
3. Touch and hold a text message. The Message options appear.
4. Touch **Delete**. A confirmation dialog appears.
5. Touch **Delete**. The message is deleted.

9. Adding Texted Phone Numbers to Contacts

A phone number contained in a text message may be immediately added to the phonebook as a new contact. To save a texted phone number as a contact:

1. Touch the icon. The Hangouts application opens.
2. Touch a conversation. The conversation opens.
3. Touch the phone number. The keypad appears with the phone number entered.
4. Touch **Add to Contacts** at the top of the screen. The Phonebook appears, as shown in **Figure 9**.
5. Touch **Create new contact**, or touch the name of an existing contact if there is already an entry for the contact. Depending on your choice, a new or existing contact screen appears.

6. Refer to *"Adding a New Contact"* on page 32 and follow the instructions to learn how to add a contact. The number contained in the text message is added to the phonebook.

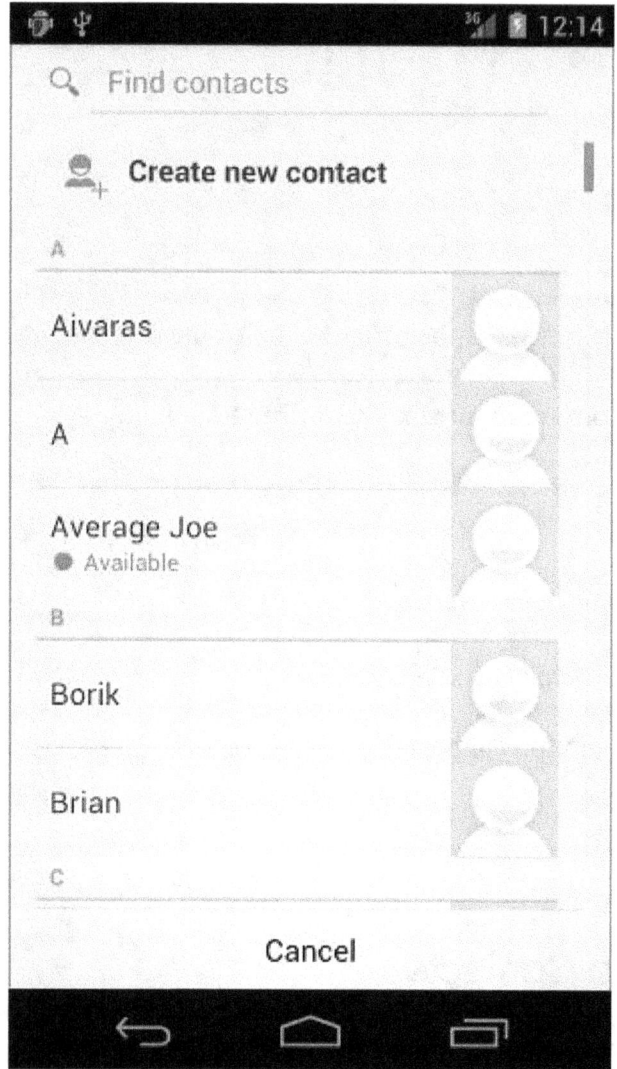

Figure 9: Phonebook

10. Attaching a Photo to a Text Message

A photo or video can be attached to any text message. To send a text message with a photo attached:

1. Refer to *"Composing a New Text Message"* on page 44 and follow steps 1-3.
2. Follow the steps in the appropriate section below:

Taking and Attaching a Photo

1. Touch the 📷 icon to the right of the text field. The Attachment Menu appears, as shown in **Figure 10**.
2. Touch **Take Photo**. The camera turns on, as shown in **Figure 11**.
3. Touch the ⊙ button. The picture is captured and displayed on the screen for review.
4. Touch the ↻ icon to retake the photo or touch the ✓ icon to attach the photo to the text message. The photo is attached and the text message appears, as shown in **Figure 12**. You can also touch the ✕ icon while previewing the photo to return to the text message without saving the captured image.

Attaching a Photo from a Photo Album

1. Touch the 📷 icon to the right of the text field. The Attachment Menu appears.
2. Touch **Attach photo**. The recently captured photos appear.
3. Touch the left side of the screen and slide your finger to the right. The Image Folder menu appears, as shown in **Figure 13**.
4. Touch **Gallery**. The Gallery appears, as shown in **Figure 14**.
5. Touch the album that contains the photo that you wish to attach. The thumbnails of the photos in the album appear.
6. Touch a photo. The photo is attached and the text message appears.

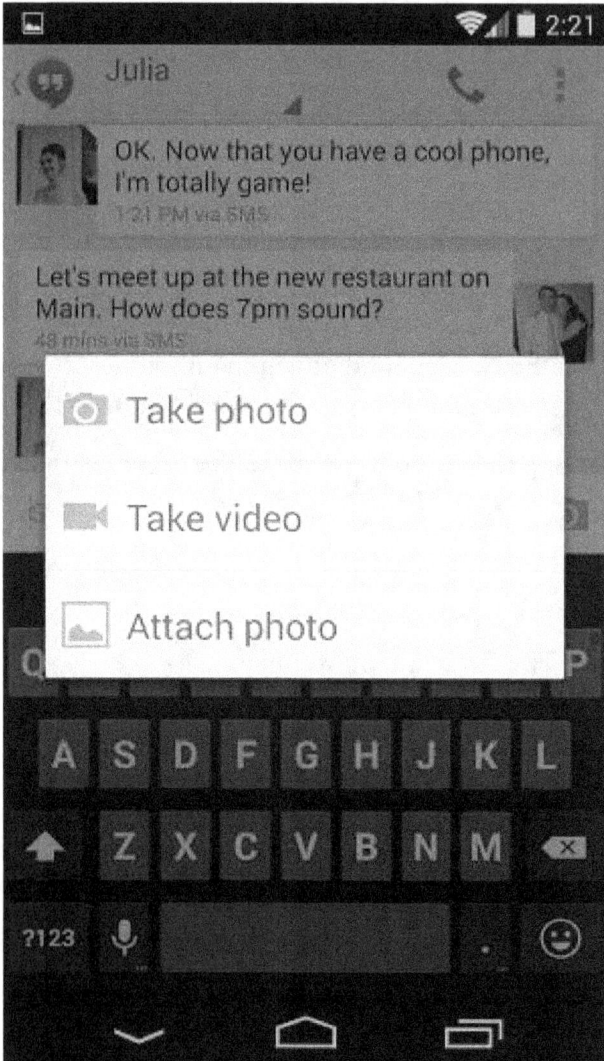

Figure 10: Attachment Menu

Figure 11: Camera Turned On

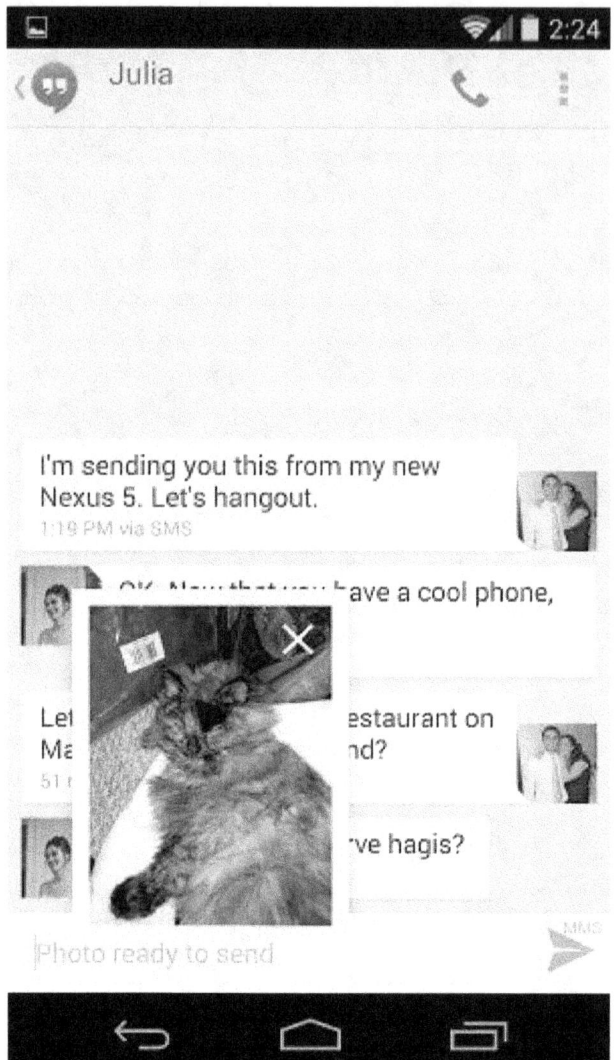

Figure 12: Text Message with Photo Attached

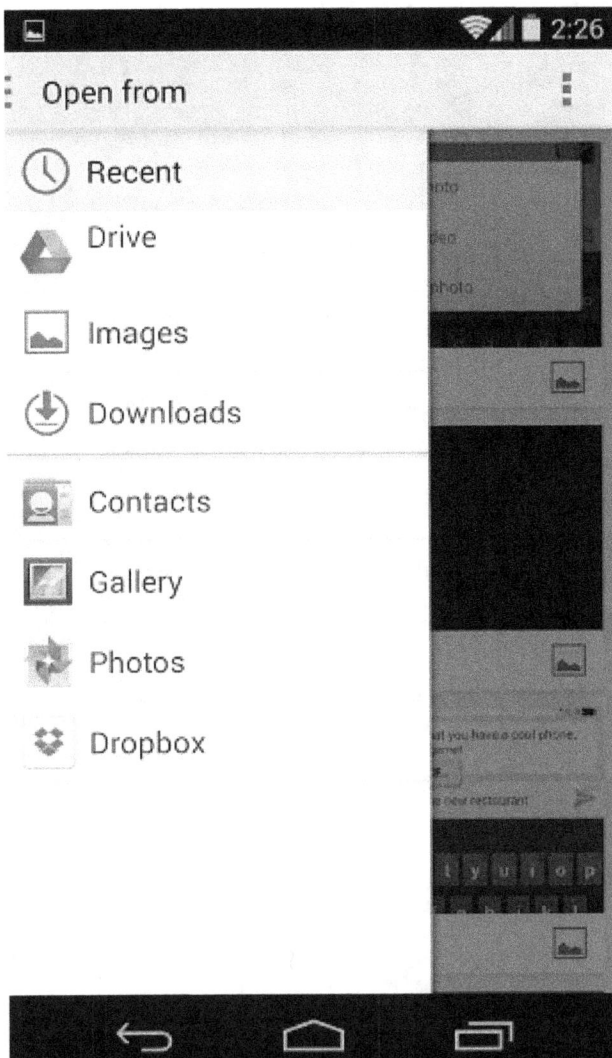

Figure 13: Image Folder Menu

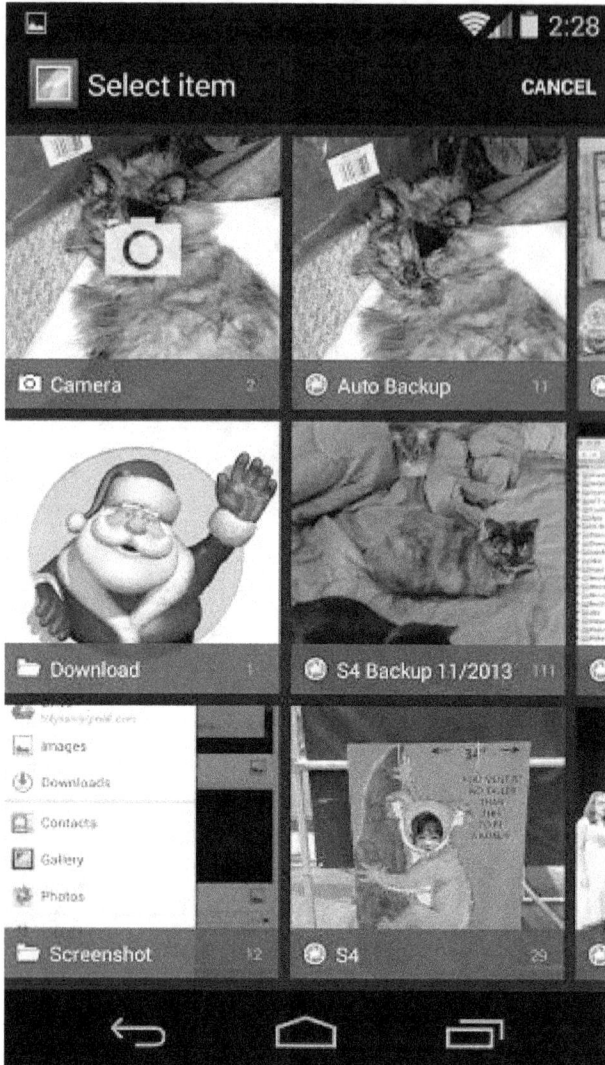

Figure 14: Gallery

11. Attaching a Video to a Text Message

The Nexus 5 can send media messages containing a video. To attach a video to a text message:

1. Refer to *"Composing a New Text Message"* on page 44 and follow steps 1-3.
2. Follow the steps in the appropriate section below:

Capturing and Attaching a Video Using the Camcorder

1. Touch the 🔘 icon to the right of the text field. The Attachment Menu appears.
2. Touch **Take video**. The camcorder turns on.

3. Touch the ⬤ button. The video begins to record.

4. Touch the ⬤ button. The camera stops recording and the preview screen appears.

5. Touch the ✖ button to discard the video and return to the text message, or touch

    the ▶ button in the center of the screen to preview it.

6. Touch the ✔ icon. The video is attached to the text message.

Attaching a Video from the Gallery

1. Touch the 📷 icon to the right of the text field. The Attachment Menu appears.
2. Touch **Attach photo**. The recently captured photos appear.
3. Touch the left side of the screen and slide your finger to the right. The Image Folder menu appears.
4. Touch **Gallery**. The Gallery appears. Thumbnails with a ▶ icon are videos.
5. Touch a video. The video is attached to the text message.

Note: An attached video cannot be longer than one minute. If the message "Video is too large for MMS message" appears, try a shorter video.

12. Saving a Photo or Video from a Text Message to Your Phone

After receiving an attachment in a text message, it can be saved to your Nexus 5. To save an attachment from a text message:

1. Touch the 💬 icon. The Hangouts application opens.
2. Touch a conversation. The conversation opens.
3. Touch the photo or video that you wish to save. The photo or video appears in full screen mode.
4. Touch the top of the video and slide your finger down. The media details appear, as shown in **Figure 15**.

5. Touch the icon in the upper right-hand corner of the screen. 'Save' appears.
6. Touch **Save**. The photo or video is saved to the Gallery.

Figure 15: Media Details

Managing Photos and Videos

Table of Contents

1. Taking a Picture

The Nexus 5 has a rear-facing eight-megapixel camera with auto focus and a front-facing 1.3 megapixel camera. To take a picture, touch the icon. The camera turns on, as shown in **Figure 1**. Touch the icon and then touch the icon to switch between cameras.

Touch a part of the screen to make the camera focus on that location. Touch the button. The picture is captured and stored in the 'Camera' album.

Figure 1: Camera Turned On

2. Capturing a Video

The camera on the Nexus 5 can act as a camcorder. To capture video:

1. Touch the ⬤ icon. The camera turns on.

2. Touch the 🔲 icon. The Camera Type menu appears.

3. Touch the 🔳 icon. The camcorder turns on.

4. Touch the ⬤ icon. The video begins to record.

5. Touch the ⬤ icon. The camera stops recording and the video is stored in the Gallery.

3. Using the Digital Zoom

While taking pictures, use the camera's built-in Digital Zoom feature if the subject of the photo is far away. Digital Zoom can also be used while recording a video. To zoom in, touch the screen with two fingers close together, and then spread them apart. To zoom out, touch the screen with two fingers spread apart, and bring them together, as if you are pinching.

Note: Because of its digital nature, the zoom function will not provide the best resolution, and the image may look fuzzy. It is recommended to be as close as possible to the subject of the photo or video.

4. Using the Flash

The Nexus 5 has a built-in LED flash, which can be used along with the rear-facing camera. When shooting a video with the flash turned on, it will remain on. To use the flash, make sure that the

camera is running. Touch the 🔘 icon. The Camera settings appear, as shown in **Figure 2**.

Touch the 🔳 icon and then touch one of the following icons:

🔳 - The flash is turned on and will be used every time a picture is taken.

🔳 - The flash is turned off and will never be used.

🔳 - The flash is set to automatic and the phone determines whether it is used based on the current lighting conditions.

Figure 2: Camera Settings

5. Browsing Pictures and Videos

Pictures can be browsed without activating the camera. To view saved images:

1. Touch the ![icon] icon. The Gallery opens, as shown in **Figure 3**.
2. Touch an album. The album opens and the thumbnails of the pictures in it appear, as shown in **Figure 4**.
3. Touch a photo or video. The photo appears in full-screen mode or the video begins to play.
4. Touch the screen and move your finger to the left or right. Other photos and videos in the same album appear.

5. Touch the ⬅️ button. The thumbnails of the pictures in the current album appear.

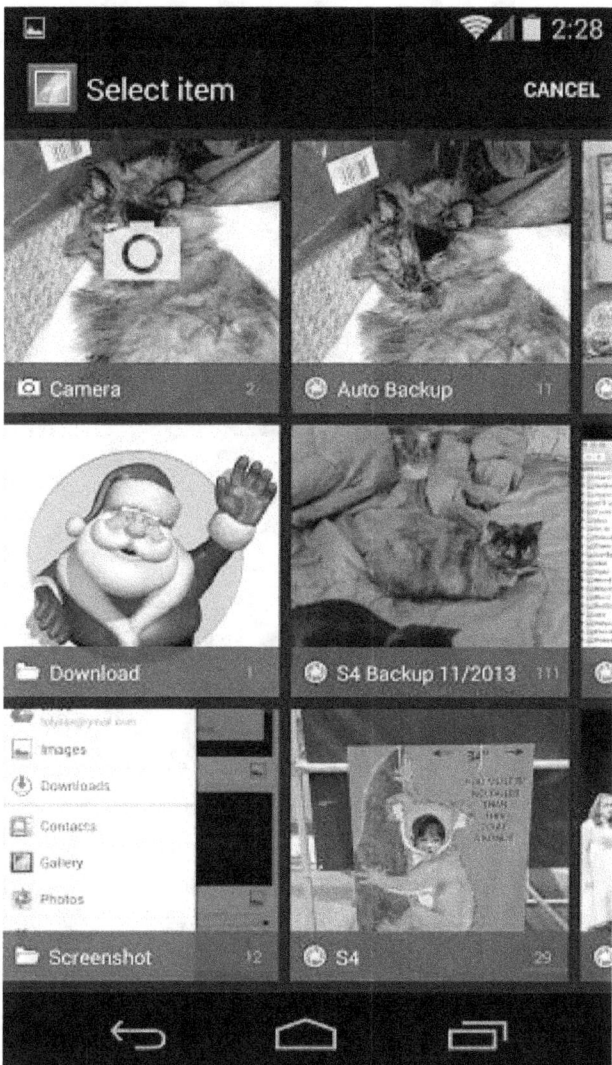

Figure 3: Gallery

Figure 4: Photo Album

6. Starting a Slideshow

The Nexus 5 can play slideshows using the pictures stored in the Gallery. To start a slideshow:

1. Touch the ⬜ icon. The Gallery opens.
2. Touch an album. The album opens.
3. Touch the ⚫ icon in the upper right-hand corner of the screen. The Album menu appears, as shown in **Figure 5**.
4. Touch **Slideshow**. The slideshow begins.
5. Touch the screen anywhere. The slideshow ends and the album thumbnails reappear.

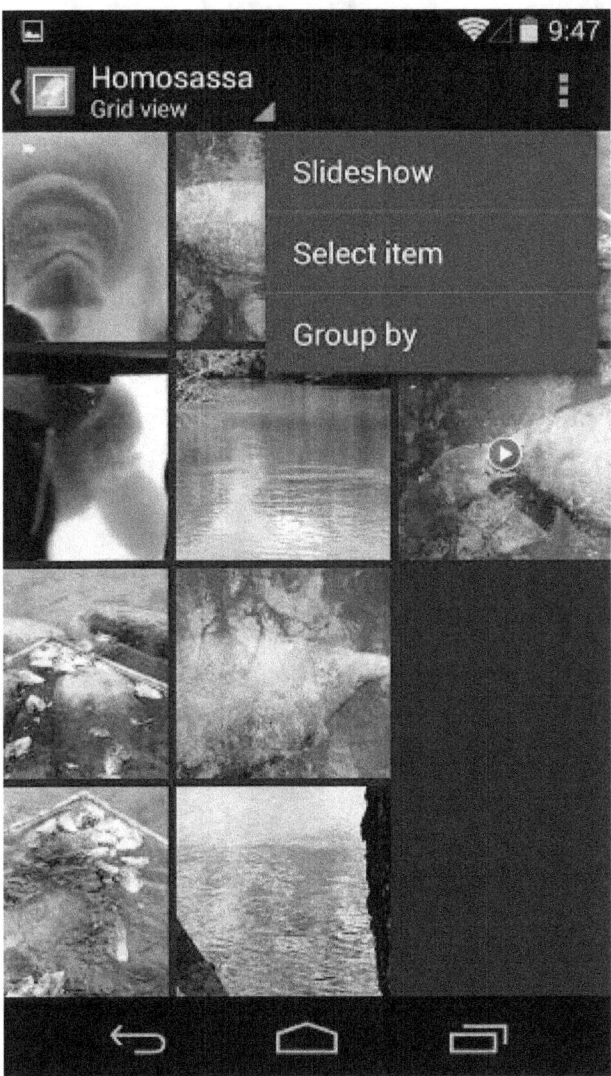

Figure 5: Album Menu

7. Editing a Photo

After taking a photo, you can use the Nexus 5 to crop it, rotate it, or enhance it with effects. To edit photos in the Gallery:

1. Touch the ▧ icon. The Gallery opens.
2. Touch an album. The album opens.
3. Touch a photo. The photo appears in full-screen mode.
4. Touch the ⋮ icon in the upper right-hand corner of the screen. The Photo menu appears, as shown in **Figure 6**.
5. Touch **Edit**. The photo is opened for photo editing, as shown in **Figure 7**.
6. Follow the steps in one of the following sections to edit the photo:

Adding Effects

To add effects to a photo, touch the ⊛ icon under the photo, and then touch the desired effect. The effect is applied. Touch **Save** in the upper left-hand corner of the screen. The new photo is saved as a copy in the 'Edited' album. The original photo is left in its original location.

Cropping a Photo

Crop a photo to use only a portion of it. To crop a photo:

1. Touch the ⌗ icon under the photo. The Photo Editing options appear, as shown in **Figure 8**.
2. Touch the ⌗ icon. A white rectangle appears on the photo.
3. Touch the ◯ icons and drag them in any direction to change the size of the cropped area. Touch inside the cropped area and move it to select the part of the photo you wish to keep.
4. Touch the ✓ icon in the bottom right-hand corner of the screen. The photo is cropped.
5. Touch **Save** in the upper right-hand corner of the screen when you are finished. The photo is saved to the 'Edited' album. The original photo is left in its original location.

Straightening a Photo

You may wish to straighten a crooked image. To straighten a photo:

1. Touch the ⬚ icon under the photo. The Photo Editing options appear.
2. Touch the ⬚ icon. Photo straightening is enabled and a grid appears for guidance.
3. Touch the screen and move your finger in any direction. The photo is reoriented accordingly.
4. Touch the ✓ icon in the bottom right-hand corner of the screen. The photo is straightened.
5. Touch **Save** in the upper left-hand corner of the screen when you are finished. The photo is saved to the 'Edited' album. The original photo is left in its original location.

Rotating a Photo

Sometimes you may wish to rotate a photo to orient it vertically or horizontally. To rotate a photo:

1. Touch the ⬚ icon under the photo. The Photo Editing options appear.
2. Touch the ↻ icon. The photo is rotated 90 degrees to the right. Keep touching the ↻ icon to rotate the photo.
3. Touch **Save** in the upper left-hand corner of the screen when you are finished. The photo is saved to the 'Edited' album. The original photo is left in its original location.

Flipping a Photo

Flipping a photo generates a mirror image of the original. To flip a photo:

1. Touch the ⬚ icon under the photo. The Photo Editing options appear.
2. Touch the ⬚ icon. The photo is flipped. Keep touching the ⬚ icon to flip the photo.
3. Touch **Save** in the upper left-hand corner of the screen when you are finished. The photo is saved to the 'Edited' album. The original photo is left in its original location.

Editing the Features of a Photo

You may edit each subtle feature of a photo, such as its exposure, contrast, or shadows. To edit the features of a photo, touch the ⊘ icon under the photo, and then touch one of the filters that appear. Use the sliders to adjust the intensity of the feature.

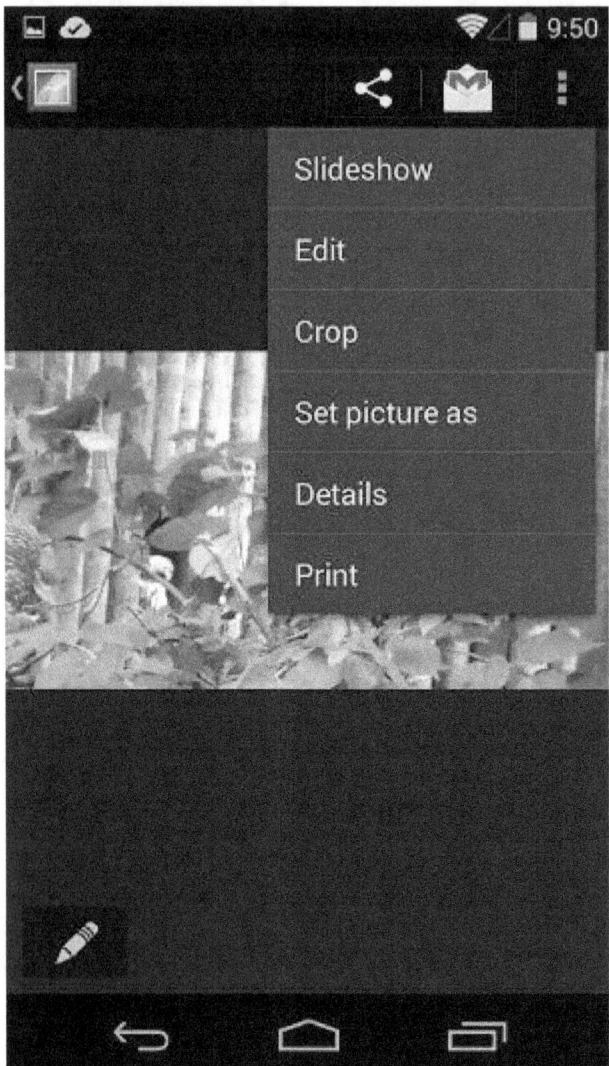

Figure 6: Photo Menu

Figure 7: Photo Open for Editing

Figure 8: Photo Editing Options

8. Deleting Pictures

Warning: Once a picture is deleted, there is no way to restore it, so make sure that you do not want the selected photos.

To free up some space in the phone's memory, try deleting pictures or videos from the Gallery. To delete a picture or video:

1. Touch the ▢ icon. The Gallery opens.
2. Touch an album. The album opens.

3. Touch and hold a picture or video. The item is selected and highlighted in blue.
4. Touch as many photos and videos as desired. The items are selected, as shown in **Figure 9**.
5. Touch the 🗑 icon in the upper right-hand corner of the screen. A confirmation dialog appears.
6. Touch **Delete**. The selected items are deleted.

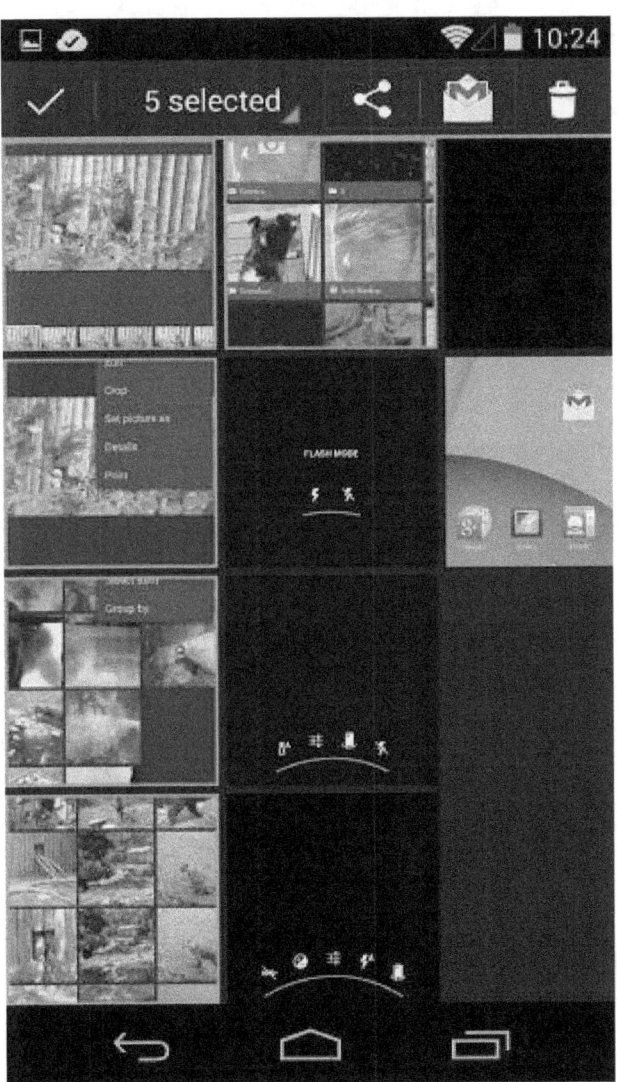

Figure 9: Selecting Photos for Deletion

Using the Chrome Browser

Table of Contents

1. Navigating to a Web Page

You can surf the Web using your Nexus 5. To navigate to a Web page using a web address:

1. Touch the icon. The Chrome browser opens, as shown in **Figure 1**.
2. Touch the address bar at the top of the screen, as outlined in **Figure 1**. The address is highlighted in blue and the virtual keyboard appears.
3. Enter the web address and touch **Go**. The phone navigates to the website.

Note: Refer to "Tips and Tricks" *on page 174 to learn more about using the address bar.*

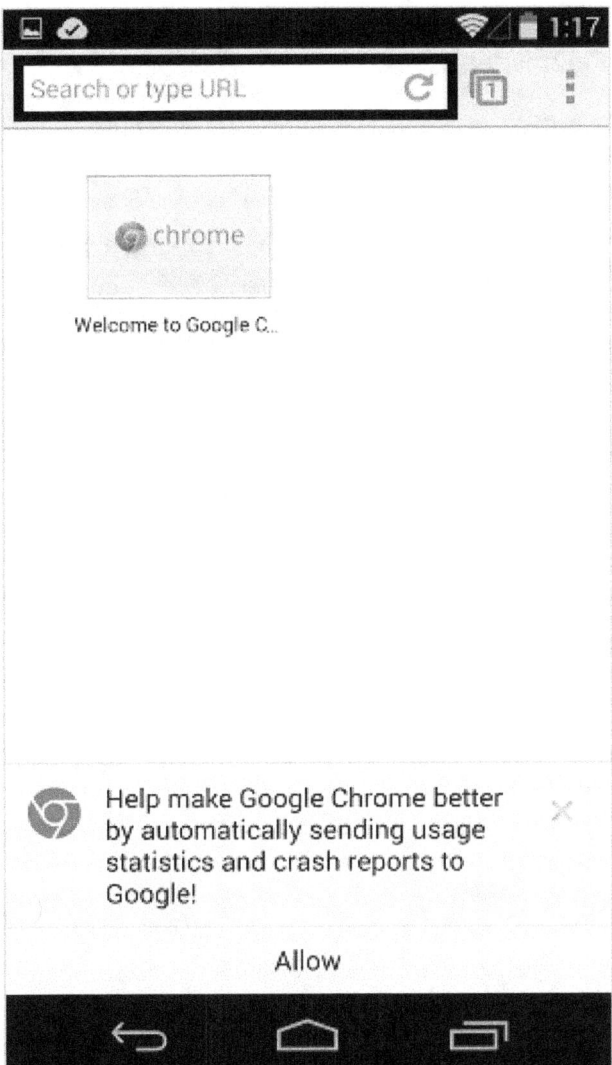

Figure 1: Chrome Browser Open

2. Adding and Viewing Bookmarks

The Nexus 5 can store favorite web pages as bookmarks to allow you to access them faster in the future. To add a bookmark:

1. Navigate to a web page. Refer to *"Navigating to a Web Page"* on page 77 to learn how.

2. Touch the ⁞ icon in the upper right-hand corner of the screen. The Browser menu appears, as shown in **Figure 2**.

3. Touch the ⭐ icon. The New Bookmark screen appears, as shown in **Figure 3**.

4. Enter a name for the bookmark. The name is entered.
5. Touch **Save**. The web page is saved to your bookmarks.

To view saved bookmarks:

1. Touch the ⋮ icon in the upper right-hand corner of the screen. The Browser menu appears.
2. Touch **Bookmarks**. A list of bookmarks appears, as shown in **Figure 4**.
3. Touch a bookmark. The browser navigates to the web page.

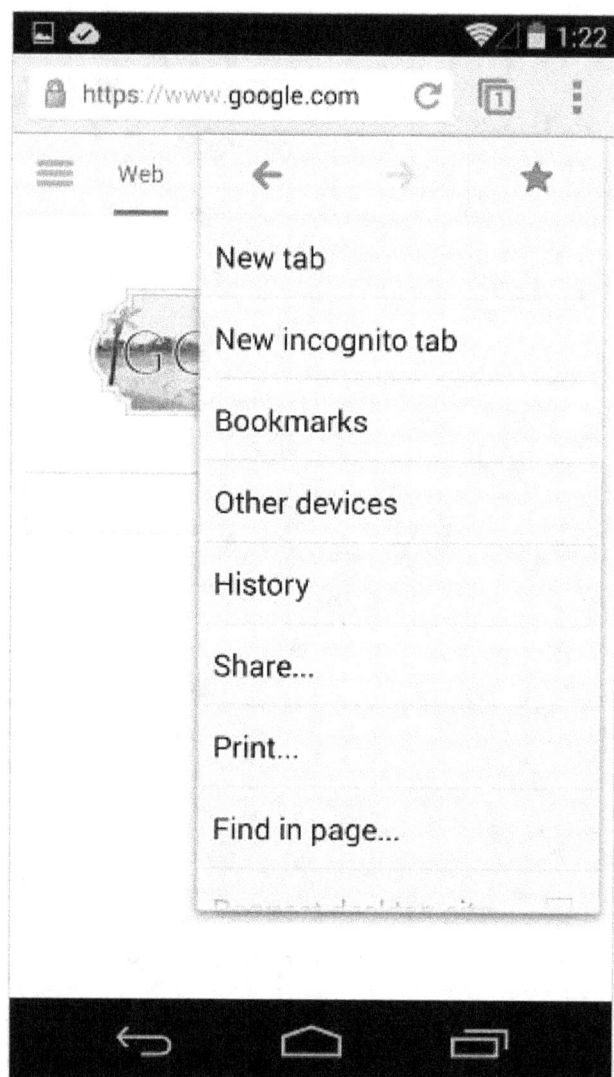

Figure 2: Browser Menu

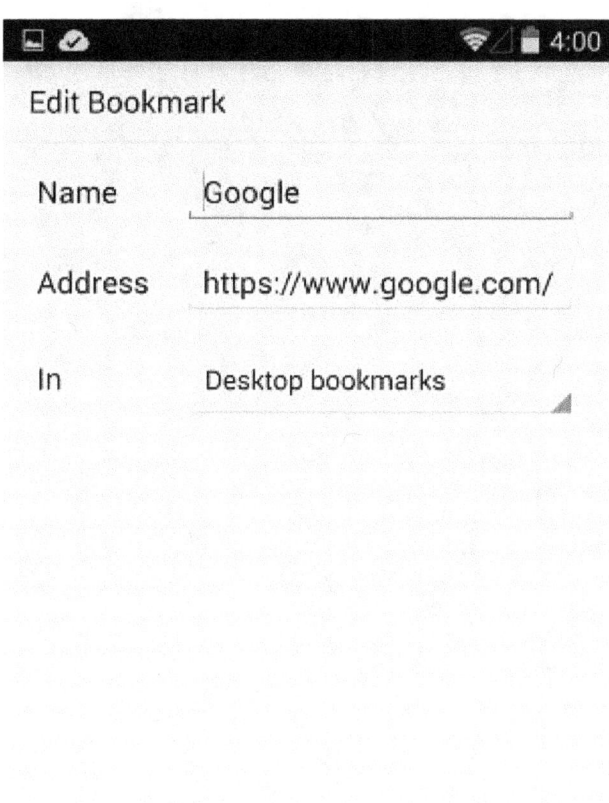

Figure 3: New Bookmark Screen

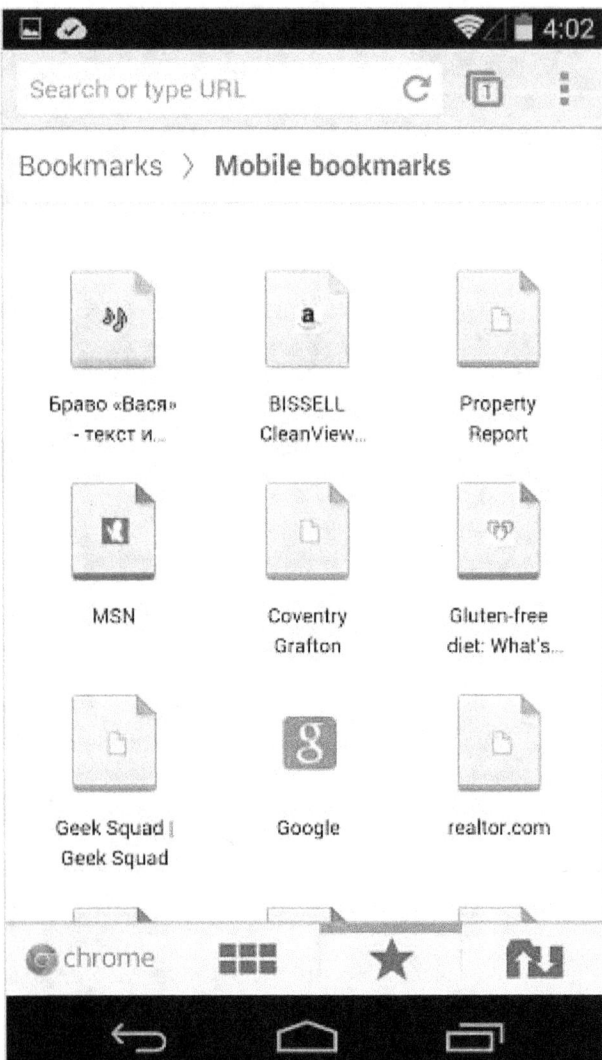

Figure 4: List of Bookmarks

3. Managing Open Browser Tabs

Tabs are like separate open browser windows, where opening a new site in one does not disrupt the other open tabs. The Chrome browser supports an unlimited number of tabs. Use the following tips when working with open tabs:

- Touch the 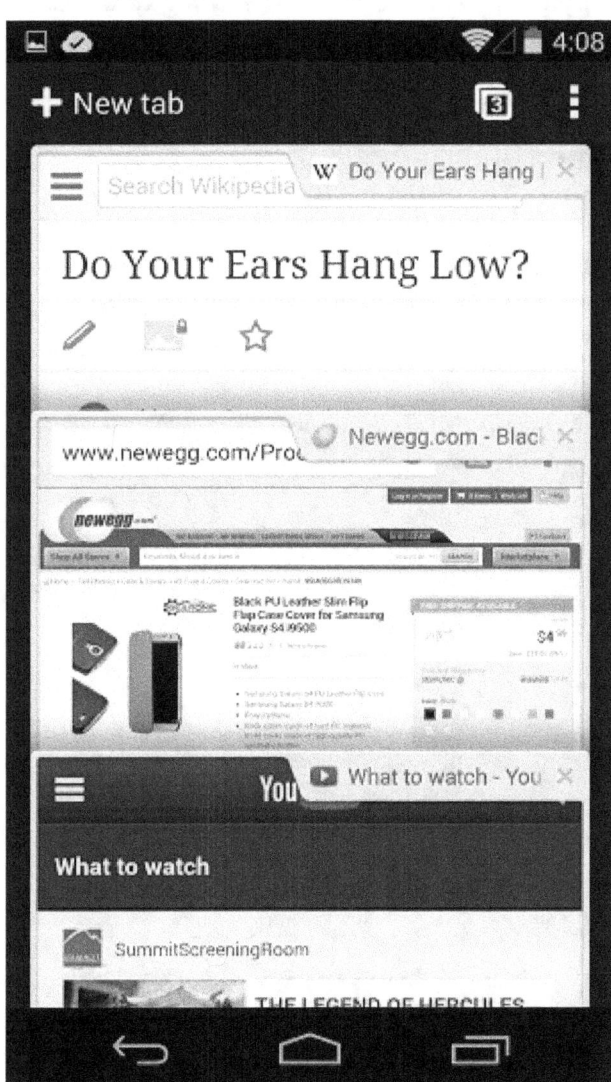 icon at the top of the Chrome browser. The open browser windows appear, as shown in **Figure 5**.
- Touch **New tab** to open a new tab.
- Touch a tab and slide it to the left or right to close it.
- Touch a tab to open it.

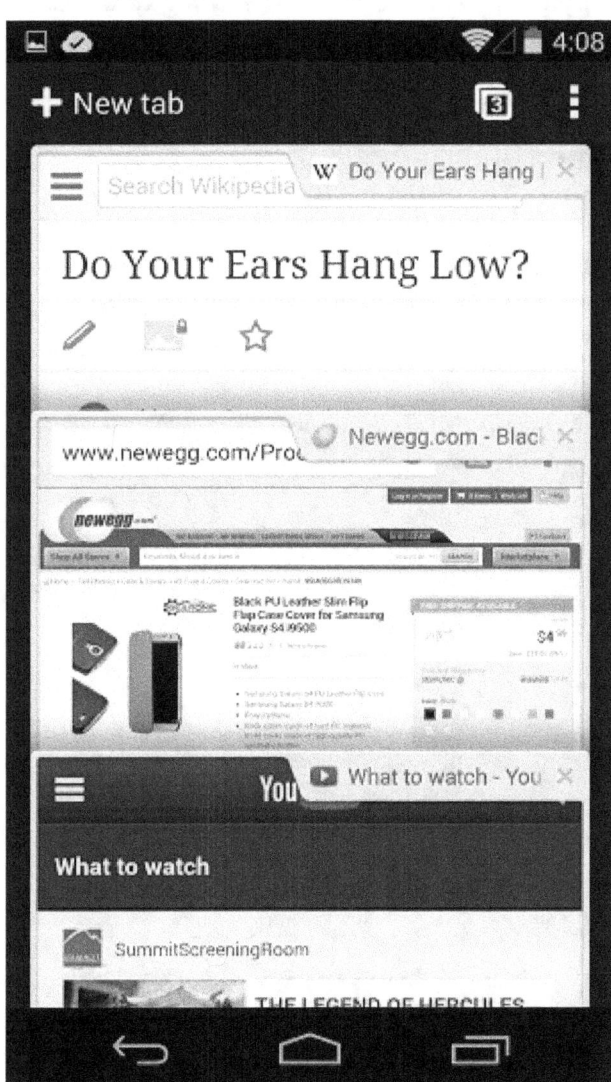

Figure 5: Open Browser Windows

4. Selecting Links and Text

In addition to touching a link to navigate to its destination, there are other link options. Touch and hold a link to see all of the link options, as shown in **Figure 6**. The following options are available:

- **Open in new tab -** Opens the link in a new tab, so as not lose the current web page. Refer to *"Managing Open Browser Tabs"* on page 81 to learn how to view all open tabs. If there are already 16 open browser tabs, choosing this option will overwrite the 16th tab.
- **Open in incognito tab** - Opens the link in a new tab, where your browsing history will not be recorded in order to preserve your privacy.
- **Copy link address** - Copies the web address to the clipboard. Touch and hold an empty space in any application and touch **Paste** to copy the link. Refer to *"Navigating to a Web Page"* on page 77 to learn how to go to a website using the URL.
- **Copy Link Text -** Selects the text in the link to be copied and pasted in another location. Refer to *"Copying, Cutting, and Pasting Text"* on page 48 to learn more. You can also touch and hold plain text to achieve the same effect.
- **Save Link** - Downloads the web page to the phone. To view a list of downloads, touch the ⊕ button at the bottom of the Home screen and touch the ⬇ icon. The Downloads screen appears, as shown in **Figure 7**. Touch a web page in the list. The Web browser opens and navigates to the Web page.

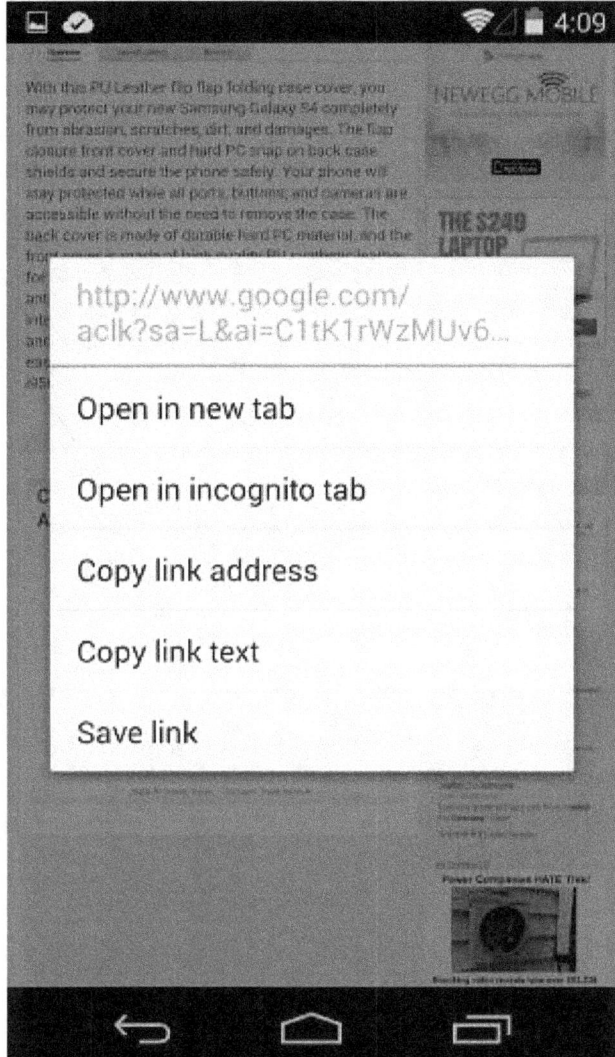

Figure 6: Link Options

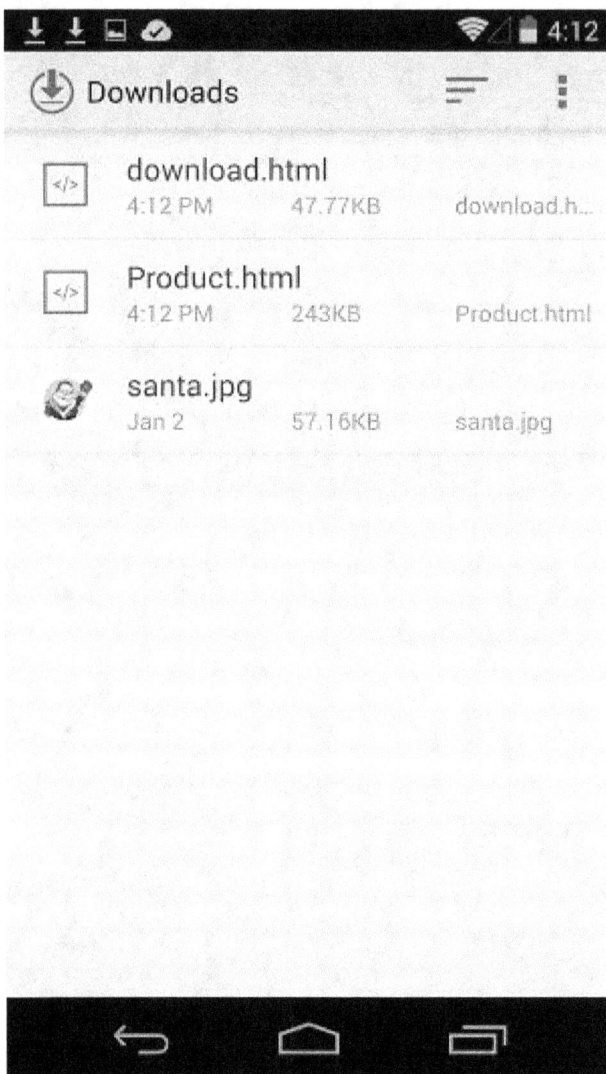

Figure 7: Downloads Screen

5. Searching a Web Page for a Word or Phrase

While surfing the Web, any page can be searched for a word or phrase. To perform a search on a web page:

1. Touch the ⋮ icon in the upper right-hand corner of the screen. The Browser menu appears.
2. Touch **Find in page**. The virtual keyboard appears.

3. Enter the search term or phrase. The results are highlighted in orange on the web page as you type, as shown in **Figure 8**. Alternatively, '0/0' appears at the top of the screen if no matches are found.

Figure 8: Search Results on Web Page

6. Viewing Recently Visited Websites

The Nexus 5 stores all recently visited websites in its History. To view the Browsing History while using the Chrome browser, touch the ⋮ icon in the upper right-hand corner of the screen. The Browser menu appears. Touch **History**. The Browsing history appears, as shown in **Figure 9**.

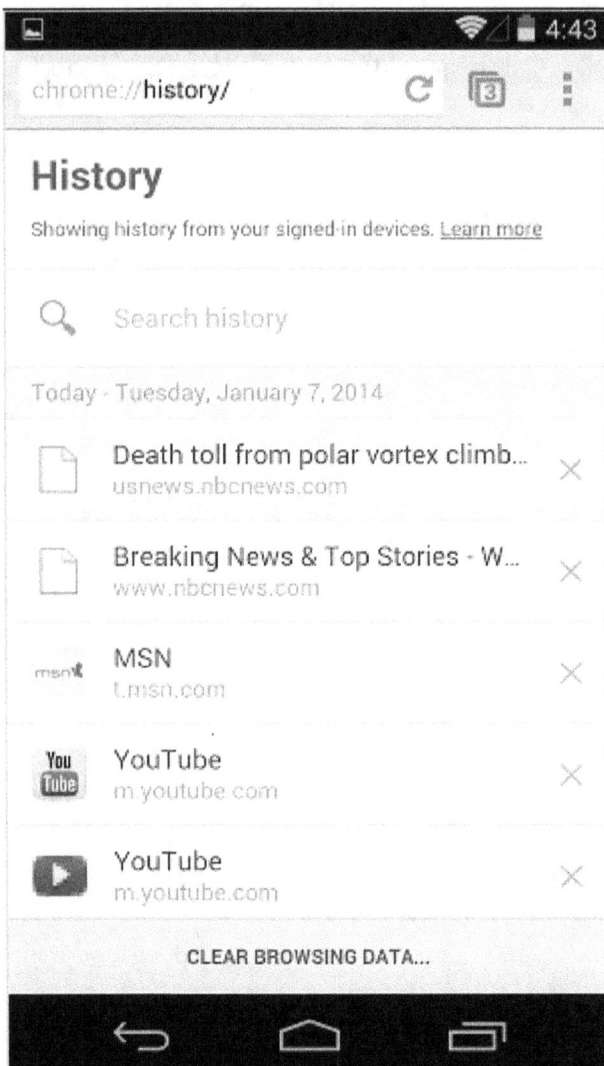

Figure 9: Browsing History

7. Clearing Personal Data

The Nexus 5 can clear personal data, such as the list of recently visited websites, known as the History. The phone can also clear other data, such as saved passwords, known as Cookies. To clear personal data while using the Web browser:

1. Touch the ▮ icon in the upper right-hand corner of the screen. The Browser menu appears.
2. Touch **Settings**. The Browser Settings screen appears.
3. Touch **Privacy**. The Privacy Settings screen appears, as shown in **Figure 10**.
4. Touch **Clear Browsing Data** at the bottom of the screen. The Browsing Data dialog appears, as shown in **Figure 11**.
5. Touch one of the following options to select the corresponding data to be deleted:

   - **Clear browsing history** - Deletes all history files, which include the addresses of recently visited websites.
   - **Clear the cache** - Deletes all web page data, such as image files and other files that comprise a web page.
   - **Clear cookies, site data** - Deletes all text data, such as site preferences, authentication, or shopping cart contents.
   - **Clear saved passwords** - Deletes all stored passwords for various websites, such as online email clients, marketplaces, and banking clients.
   - **Clear autofill data -** Deletes all form data, such as screen names, addresses, and phone numbers.

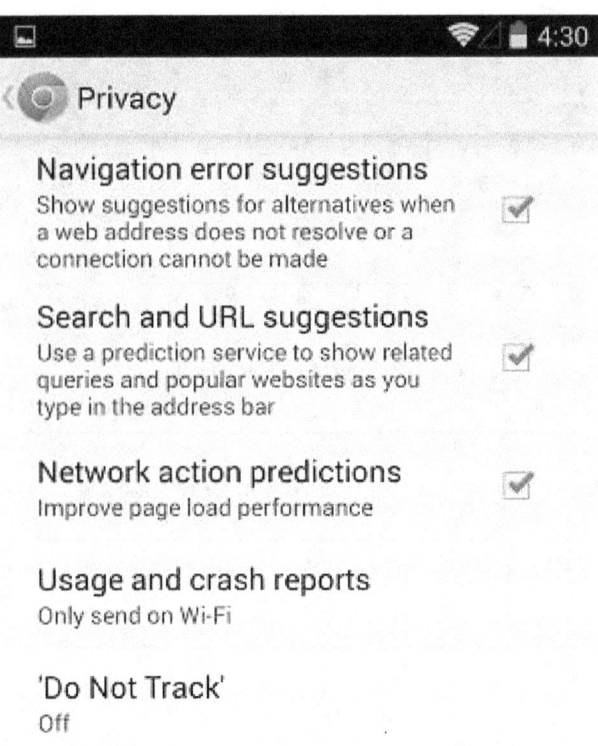

Figure 10: Privacy Settings Screen

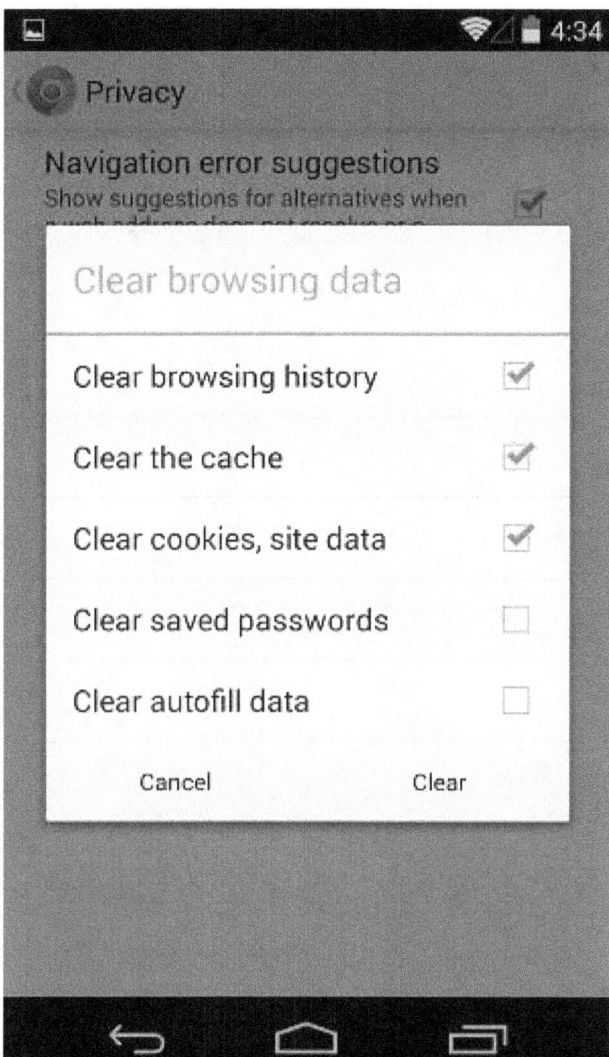

Figure 11: Browsing Data Dialog

Using the Gmail Application

Table of Contents

1. Adding a Google Account to the Phone

Before using the Gmail application, add at least one Google account to the Nexus 5. It is highly recommended to use the Gmail service with the phone, since a Google account is required to use the Play store anyway. To add a Google account to the phone:

1. Touch the icon at the bottom of the Home screen. The Application screen appears, as shown in **Figure 1**.
2. Touch the screen and move your finger to the left. The second page of applications appears.
3. Touch the icon. The Settings screen appears, as shown in **Figure 2**.
4. Touch **Add account** under 'Accounts'. The Add Account screen appears, as shown in **Figure 3**.
5. Touch **Google**. The Google accounts screen appears.
6. Touch **Existing**. The Sign In screen appears.
7. Enter your username and password and touch **Done** in the bottom right-hand corner of the screen. The Google account is added to your phone.

*Note: To create a Google account, touch **New** in step 6. Touch each field to enter the required information. A Google account is created.*

Figure 1: Application Screen

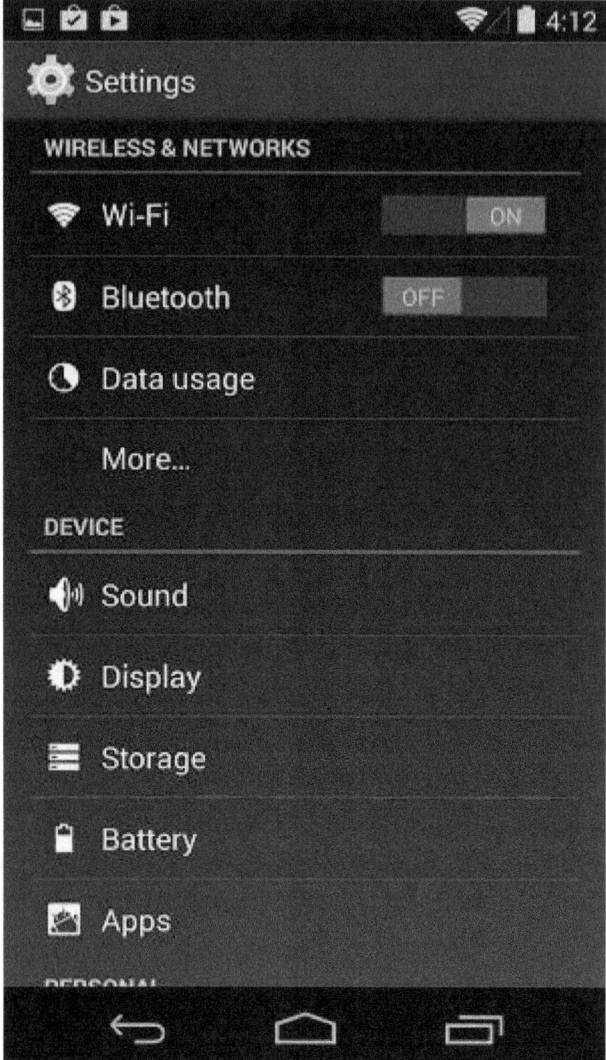

Figure 2: Settings Screen

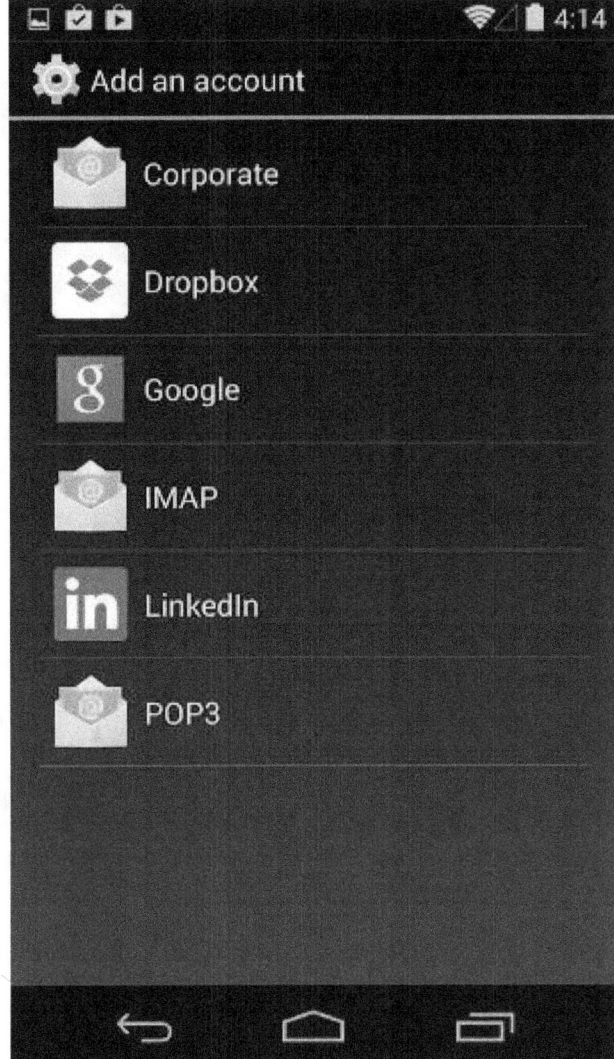

Figure 3: Add Account Screen

2. Reading Email

You can read your email on the Nexus 5 using the Gmail application. To read email:

1. Touch the ⊞ icon at the bottom of the Home screen. The Application screen appears.
2. Touch the 🅼 icon. The Gmail application opens and the Inbox appears, as shown in **Figure 4**.
3. Touch an email in the list. The email opens.

4. Touch the screen and move your finger to the left or right to view the previous or next email, respectively. The email appears.

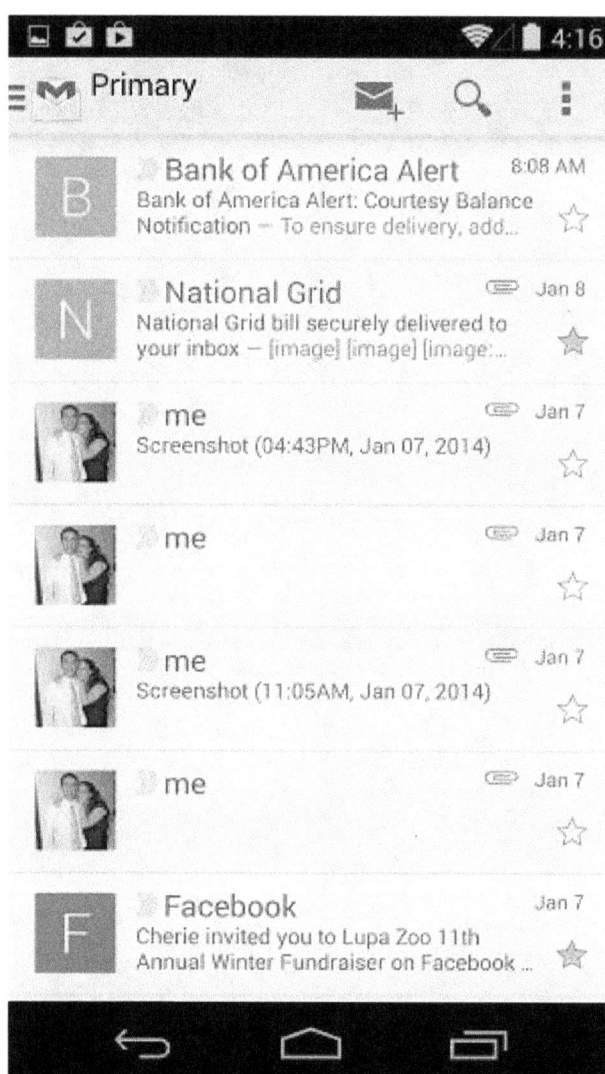

Figure 4: Gmail Inbox

3. Composing an Email

Compose email directly from the Nexus 5 using the Gmail application. To write an email while using the Gmail application:

1. Make sure you are viewing the Inbox. Refer to *"Reading Email"* on page 94 to learn how.

2. Touch the ✉ icon at the top of the screen. The New Email screen appears, as shown in **Figure 5**.

3. Start entering the name of a contact for which you have a saved email address. A list of suggestions appears.
4. Touch the contact's name. The contact's email address is inserted. Alternatively, you may enter an email from scratch in the 'To' field.
5. Touch **Subject** and enter an optional topic for the email. Touch **Compose email** and enter a message. The subject and message are entered.
6. Touch the ![send] button at the top of the screen. The email is sent.

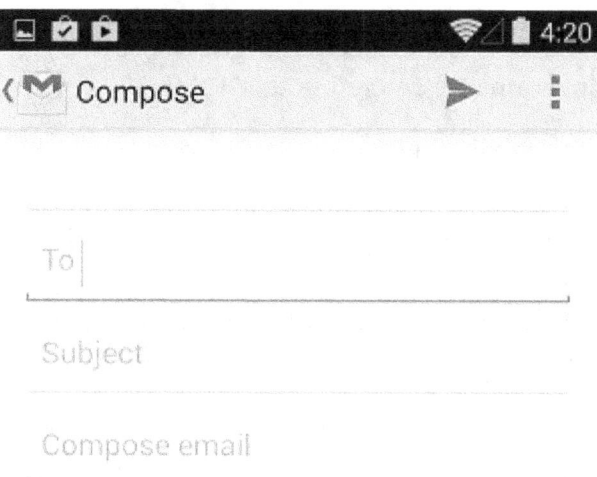

Figure 5: New Email Screen

4. Replying to and Forwarding Emails

After receiving an email, you can reply to the sender or forward the email to a new recipient. To reply to, or forward, an email while using the Gmail application:

1. Make sure that you are viewing the Inbox. Refer to *"Reading Email"* on page 94 to learn how.
2. Touch an email. The email opens.
3. Touch the ← icon next to the sender's email address, as outlined in **Figure 6**. A new email is generated with the sender's email address already entered in the 'To' field.
4. Enter a message and touch the ➤ button. The reply is sent.

5. Alternatively, touch the ⁝ icon to the right of the ← icon in step 3, and then touch **Reply all** or **Forward**. Choosing 'Reply all' will send a reply to all recipients of the original email. Choosing 'Forward' will send a copy of the message to a different recipient, requiring you to enter an email address in the 'To' field. Follow step 4 to reply to all recipients or to forward the email.

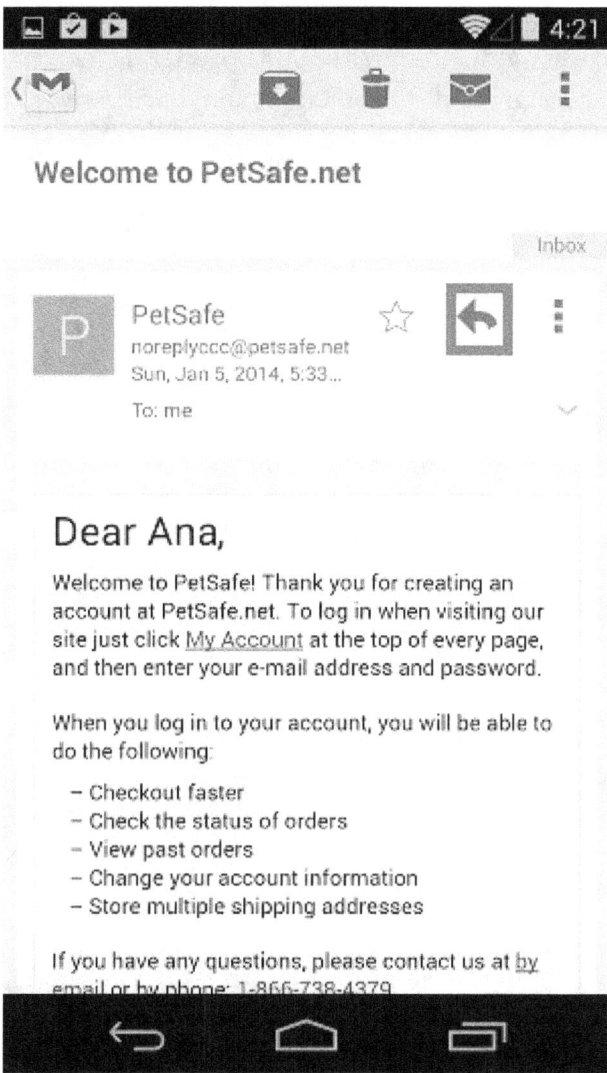

Figure 6: Reply Icon

5. Deleting Emails and Restoring Deleted Emails to the Inbox

Deleting an email sends it to the 'Trash' folder. To completely delete an email, the 'Trash' folder must be emptied. To delete emails while using the Gmail application:

1. Make sure that you are viewing the Inbox. Refer to *"Reading Email"* on page 94 to learn how.

2. Touch the letter or picture to the left of each email that you wish to delete. The emails are selected, as shown in **Figure 7**. The letter will always be the first letter of the name or service involved in the email conversation. For instance, if it is an email conversation with George, touch the icon. A picture will appear next to an email if the contact is associated with your Google+ account.

3. Touch the icon at the top of the screen. The selected emails are sent to the 'Trash' folder.

To restore deleted emails to the Inbox:

1. Make sure that you are viewing the Inbox. Refer to *"Reading Email"* on page 94 to learn how.
2. Touch your email address at the top of the screen. A list of Gmail folders appears, as shown in **Figure 8**. Touch the screen and move your finger up to scroll down the list.
3. Touch **Trash**. The Trash folder appears.
4. Touch the letter or picture to the left of each email that you wish to restore to the Inbox. The emails are selected.
5. Touch the icon at the bottom of the screen. A list of Gmail folders appears.
6. Touch **Primary**. The selected emails are restored to the main Inbox.

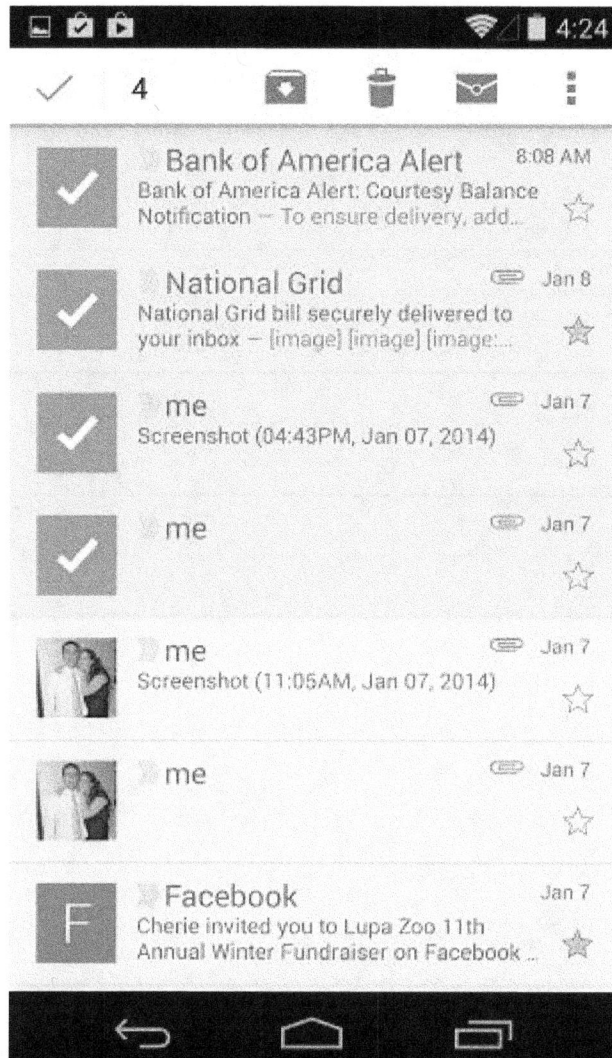

Figure 7: Selected Emails

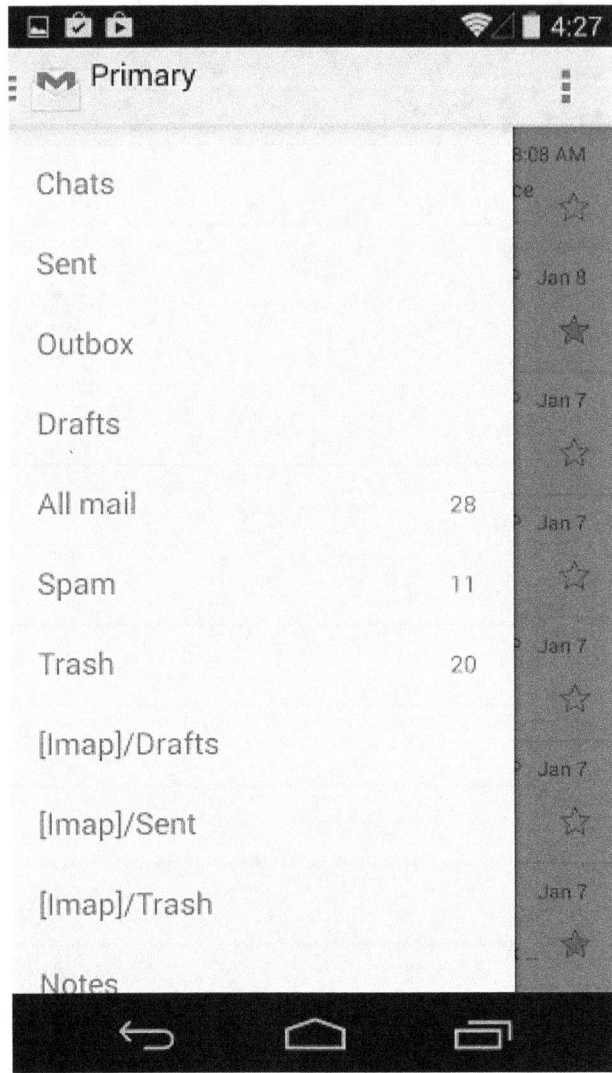

Figure 8: List of Gmail Folders

6. Adding Labels to Emails

Emails can be classified according to the nature of the message, such as 'work' or 'personal'. To add labels to emails while using the Gmail application:

1. Make sure that you are viewing the Inbox. Refer to *"Reading Email"* on page 94 to learn how.
2. Touch and hold an email. The email is selected.

3. Touch the letter or picture to the left of each email to which you wish to apply a label. This letter will always be the first letter of the name or service involved in the email conversation. For instance, if it is an email conversation with George, touch the ⬜ icon. A picture will appear next to an email if the contact is associated with your Google+ account. The emails are selected and highlighted in blue. Repeat this step for each email to which you wish to apply a label.

4. Touch the ⋮ icon in the upper right-hand corner of the screen. The Email Conversation menu appears, as shown in **Figure 9**.

5. Touch **Change Labels**. A list of available labels appears, as shown in **Figure 10**.

6. Touch as many labels as you wish to apply to the selected emails. Touch **OK**. The labels are added to the selected emails.

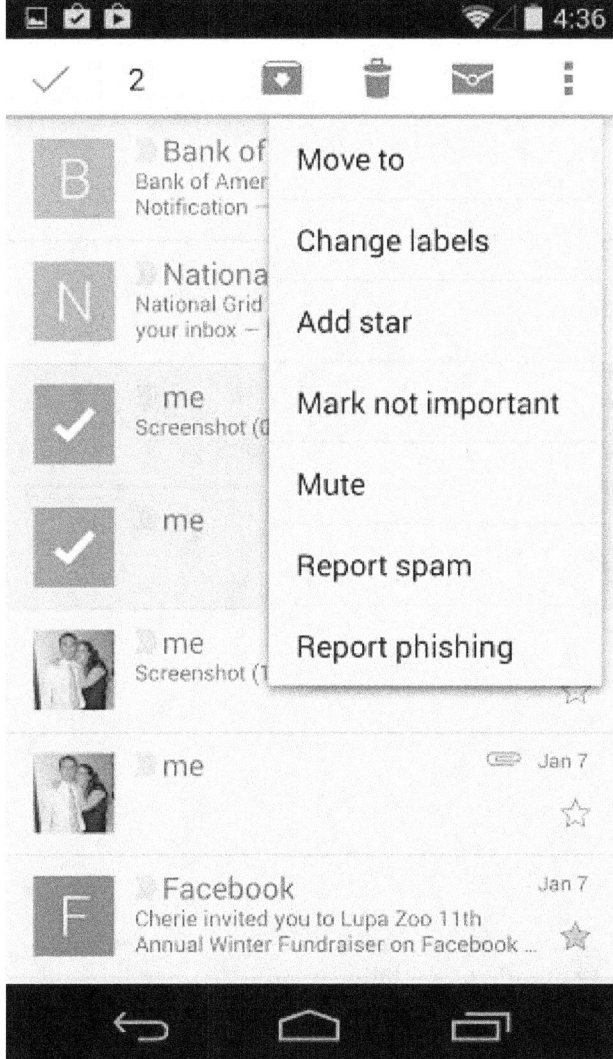

Figure 9: Email Conversation Menu

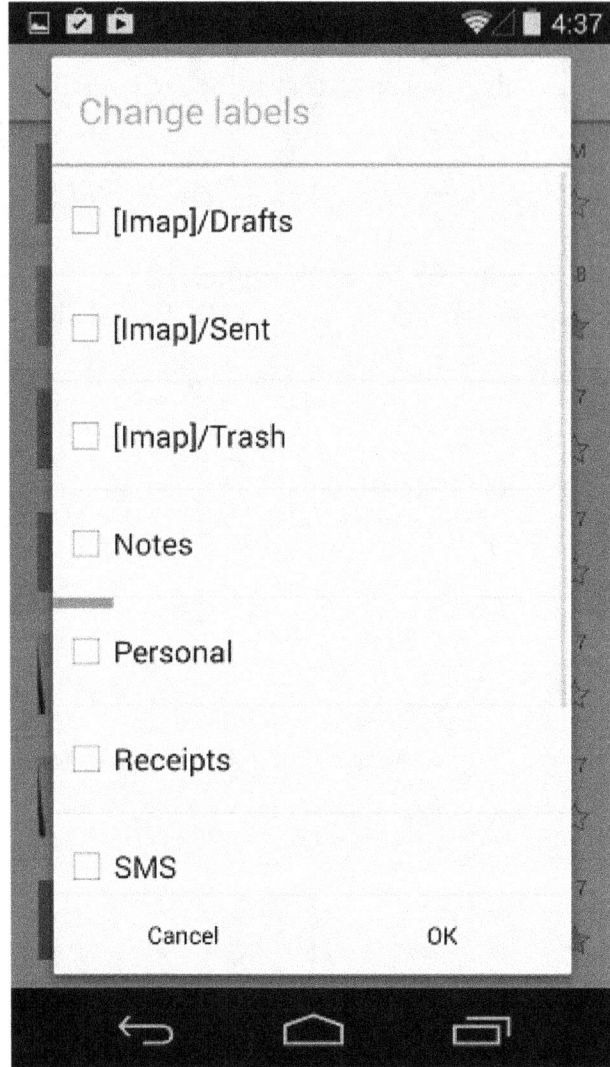

Figure 10: List of Available Labels

7. Searching the Inbox

To find an email in the Inbox, use the search function, which searches email addresses, message content, and subject lines. To search the Inbox while using the Gmail application:

1. Make sure that you are viewing the Inbox. Refer to *"Reading Email"* on page 94 to learn how.

2. Touch the search icon at the top of the screen. The virtual keyboard appears.

3. Enter a search word or phrase and touch the 🔍 button in the bottom right-hand corner of the keyboard. The Nexus 5 searches the Inbox and a list of search results appears.

8. Adjusting the General Gmail Preferences

You may customize the Gmail application by adjusting its settings. To adjust the general Gmail preferences while using the Gmail application:

1. Touch the ⋮ icon in the upper right-hand corner of the screen at any time. The Gmail menu appears.
2. Touch **Settings**. The Gmail Settings screen appears, as shown in **Figure 11**.
3. Touch **General settings**. The General Settings screen appears, as shown in **Figure 12**.
4. Touch one of the following options to adjust the corresponding setting:

   - **Confirm before deleting** - Displays a confirmation dialog before deleting an email.

     This feature is enabled when a ✓ icon appears next to 'Confirm before deleting'. Refer to *"Deleting Emails and Restoring Deleted Emails to the Inbox"* on page 98 to learn how to delete an email.
   - **Confirm before archiving** - Displays a confirmation dialog before archiving an email.

     This feature is enabled when a ✓ icon appears next to 'Confirm before archiving'.
   - **Confirm before sending** - Displays a confirmation dialog before sending an email.

     This feature is enabled when a ✓ icon appears next to 'Confirm before sending'. Refer to *"Composing an Email"* on page 95 to learn more about sending email.
   - **Reply all** - Turns the ↩ icon, used by default to reply only to the original sender, into a 'Reply all' icon, which is used to reply to all recipients of the email by default.

     This feature is enabled when a ✓ icon appears next to 'Reply all'. Refer to *"Replying to and Forwarding Emails"* on page 97 to learn more. When this feature is turned on, touch the ⋮ icon to the right of the ↩ icon and then touch **Reply** to reply only to the original sender.
   - **Auto-advance** - Selects the screen that is displayed after deleting an open email. Touch **Auto-advance**, and then touch either **Newer conversation**, **Older conversation**, or **Conversation list** to select the next screen that will be displayed.

- **Message Actions** - Pins the message actions in a blue bar at the top of the screen when scrolling through an email. Touch **Message Actions**, and then touch **Always show**, **Only show in portrait**, or **Don't show** to select when the message actions should remain pinned at the top of the screen.
- **Auto-fit messages -** Automatically shrinks messages when they are too wide to fit on the screen. This feature is enabled when a 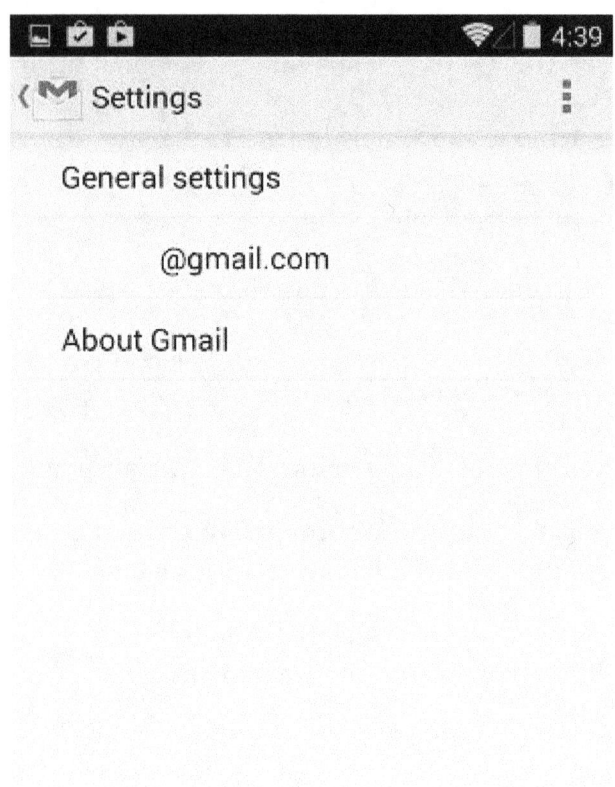 icon appears next to 'Confirm before sending'.
- **Sender image** - Turns the image of the sender that appears to the left of each email in the Inbox on or off.

Figure 11: Gmail Settings Screen

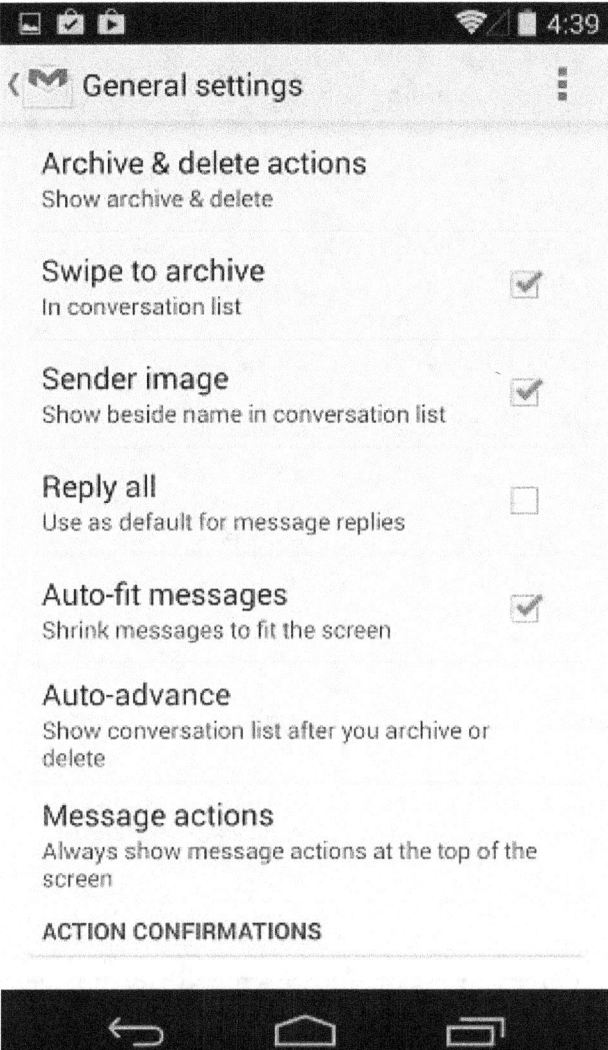

Figure 12: General Settings Screen

9. Adjusting Gmail Account Preferences

You may adjust the settings particular to your Gmail account. To adjust Gmail account preferences:

1. Touch the ⋮ icon in the upper right-hand corner of the screen at any time. The Gmail menu appears.
2. Touch **Settings**. The Gmail Settings screen appears.

3. Touch your email address. The Account Preferences screen appears, as shown in **Figure 13**.
4. Touch one of the following options to adjust the corresponding setting:

   - **Inbox type** - Set whether the Default Inbox or the Priority Inbox is the default. The Priority Inbox will only display priority emails.
   - **Inbox categories** - Set the categories that appear in the Inbox, such as 'Social' and 'Updates'. Google automatically sorts your email into these categories and displays them in separate Inboxes.
   - **Notifications** - Turn on new Email notifications. The icon appears in the upper left-hand corner of the screen when a new email arrives. A mark next to 'Notifications' signifies that the feature is on.
   - **Inbox sound** - Display the Manage Labels screen, where you can choose which mailboxes display new email notifications and select the sound that plays when a new email arrives. Touch **Sound** on the Manage Labels screen to select the Notification ringtone.
   - **Signature** - Enter a default signature that will be attached to the end of each sent email.
   - **Sync Gmail** - Turn automatic email retrieval on or off. A mark next to 'Sync Gmail' signifies that the feature is turned on.
   - **Days of mail to sync** - Choose how many days in the past the Inbox should sync. For instance, if you select '3', the Gmail application will go back three days each time it syncs the email.
   - **Manage Labels** - Brings you to the same screen as when you touch 'Ringtone & vibrate'.
   - **Download attachments** - Turn on to have Gmail automatically download any attached files. A mark next to 'Sync Gmail' signifies that the feature is turned on.

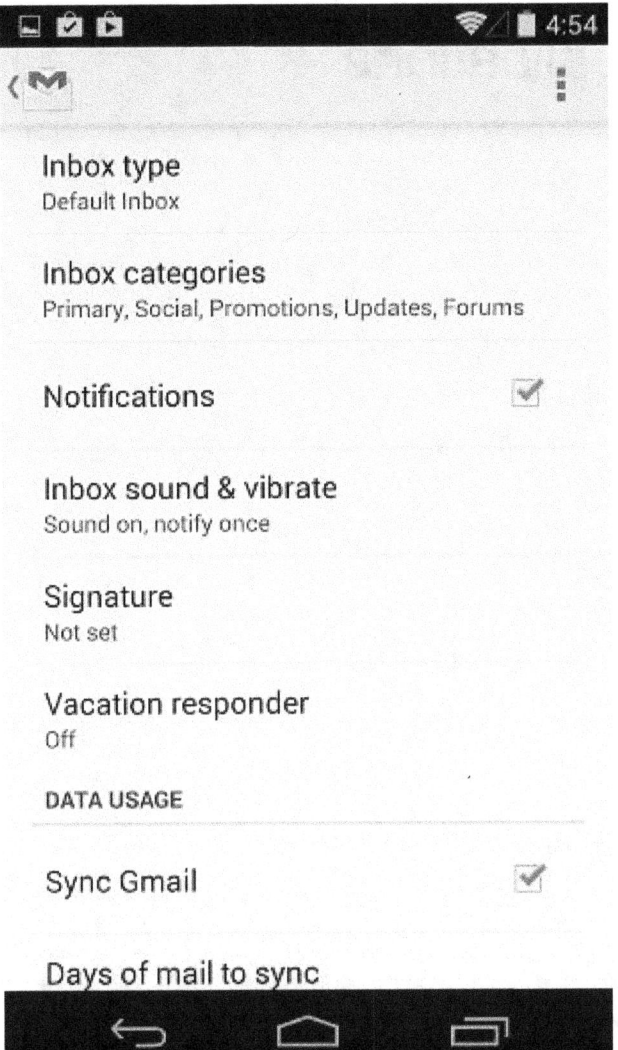

Figure 13: Account Preferences Screen

Managing Applications

Table of Contents

1. Setting Up a Google Account

In order to buy applications, you will need to assign a Google account to the Nexus 5. Refer to *"Adding a Google Account to the Phone"* on page 91 to learn how.

2. Searching for an Application

You can search for applications in the Play Store. There are two ways to search for applications:

Manual Search

To manually search for an application:

1. Touch the ⊞ icon at the bottom of the Home screen. The Application screen appears, as shown in **Figure 1**.

2. Touch the ▶ icon. The Play Store opens, as shown in **Figure 2**.

3. Touch the 🔍 icon at the top of the screen. The virtual keyboard appears.

4. Enter the name of an application or developer and then touch the button in the bottom right-hand corner of the keyboard. The matching application results appear, as shown in **Figure 3**.
5. Touch an application name. A description of the application appears.

Browse by Category

To browse applications by category:

1. Touch the icon at the bottom of the Home screen. The Application screen appears.
2. Touch the icon. The Play Store opens.
3. Touch **Apps** or **Games**. The Featured Applications screen appears, as shown in **Figure 4**.
4. Touch the screen and slide your finger to the right. The Application Categories appear, as shown in **Figure 5**.
5. Touch a category. The associated applications appear.
6. Touch an application name. A description of the application appears.

Figure 1: Application Screen

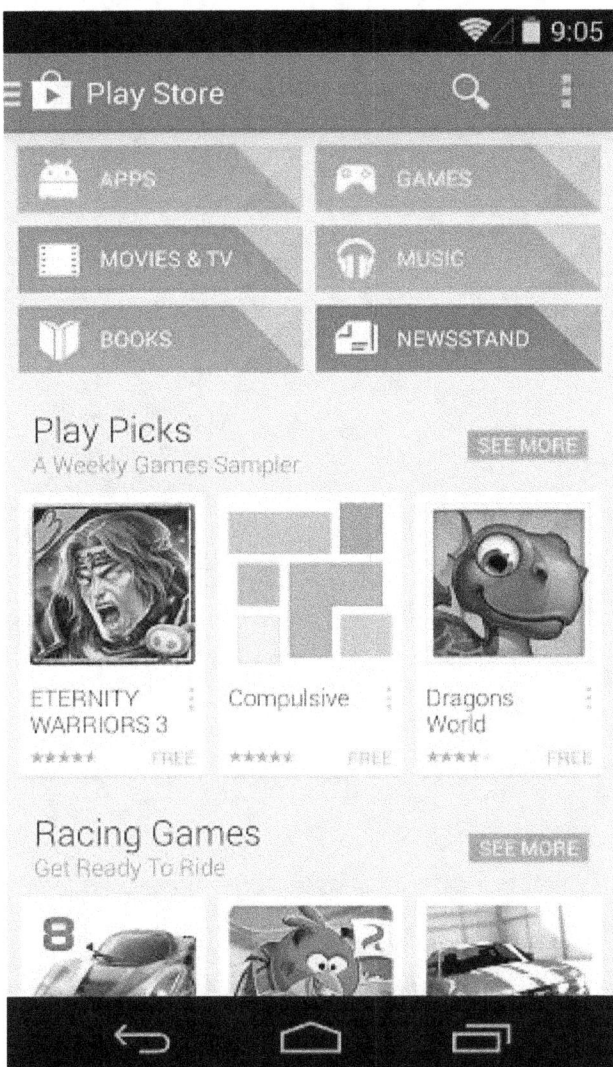

Figure 2: Play Store

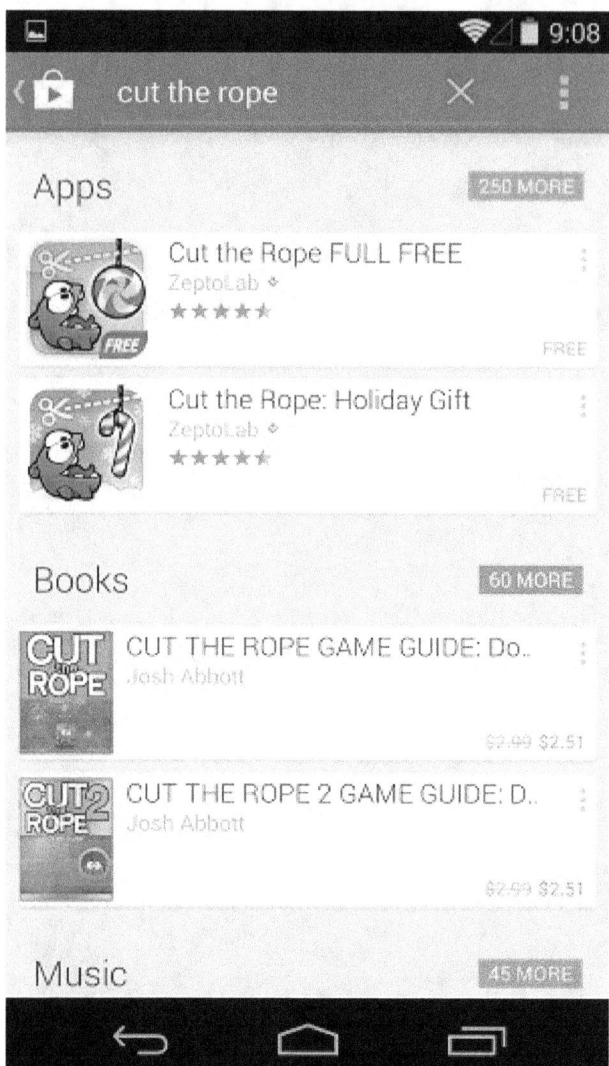

Figure 3: Matching Application Results

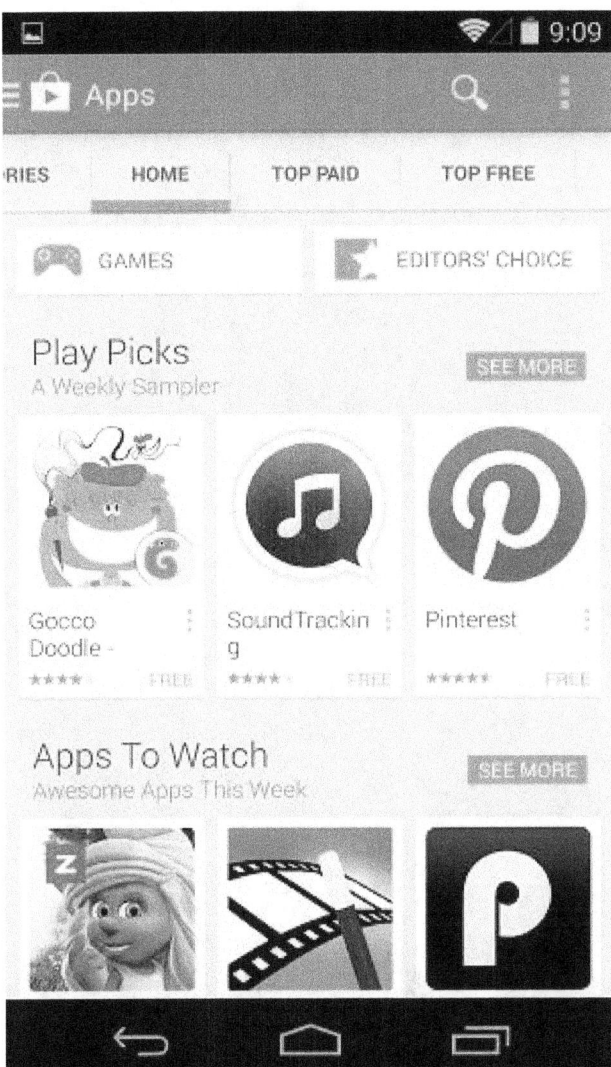

Figure 4: Featured Applications Screen

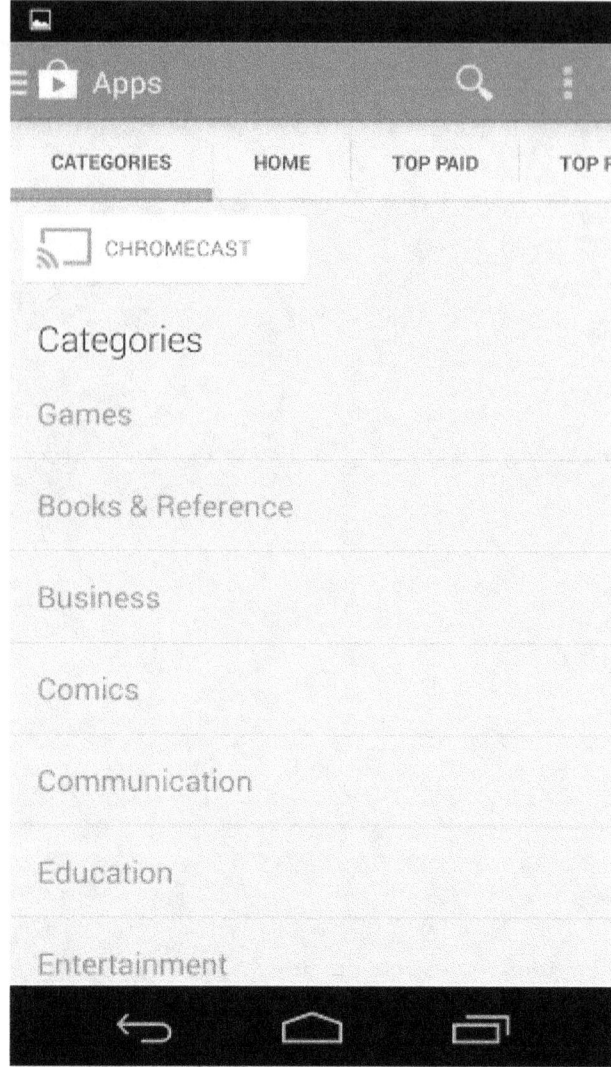

Figure 5: Application Categories

3. Buying an Application

Applications can be purchased directly from the Nexus 5 using the Android Market. To purchase an application from the Android Market:

1. Find an application. Refer to *"Searching for an Application"* on page 109 to learn how.
2. Touch an application name. The Application Description screen appears, as shown in **Figure 6**.
3. Follow the instructions below to download the application:

Installing Free Applications

Touch the [INSTALL] button. The Permissions screen appears, as shown in **Figure 7**. Touch the [ACCEPT] button. The application begins to download and the progress is shown. Touch **OPEN** to run the application when it is finished downloading and installing.

Installing Paid Applications

Touch the price of the application. The Permissions screen appears. Touch the [ACCEPT] button. The application begins to download and the progress is shown. You may also need to enter your Google password before the application can be purchased. Touch **OPEN** to run the application when it is finished downloading and installing.

Note: When purchasing an application for the first time, Google Checkout asks for your credit card information. The information is saved and used for all subsequent purchases.

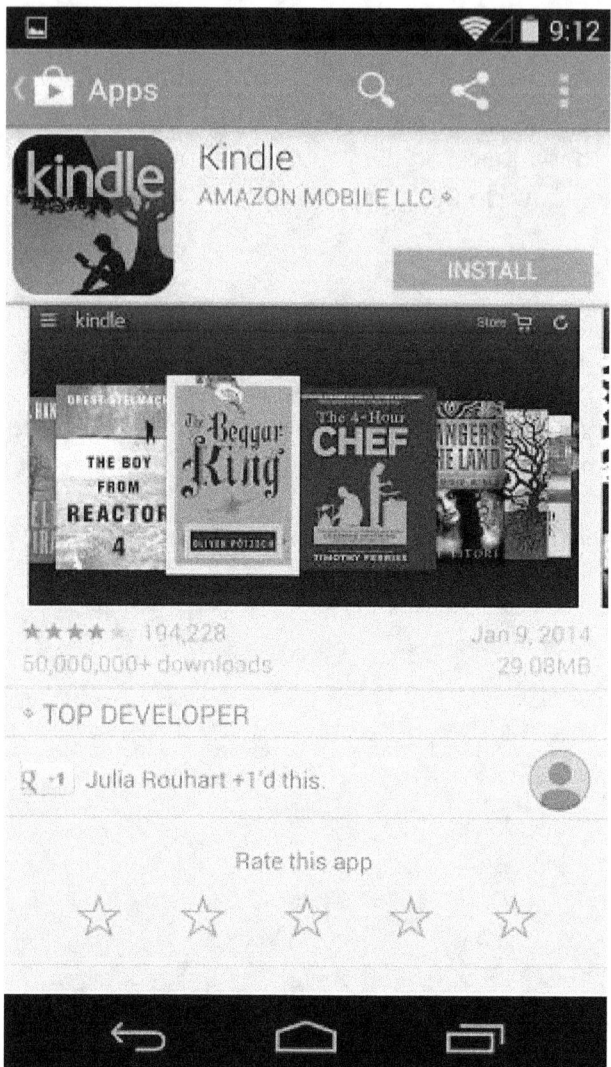

Figure 6: Application Description

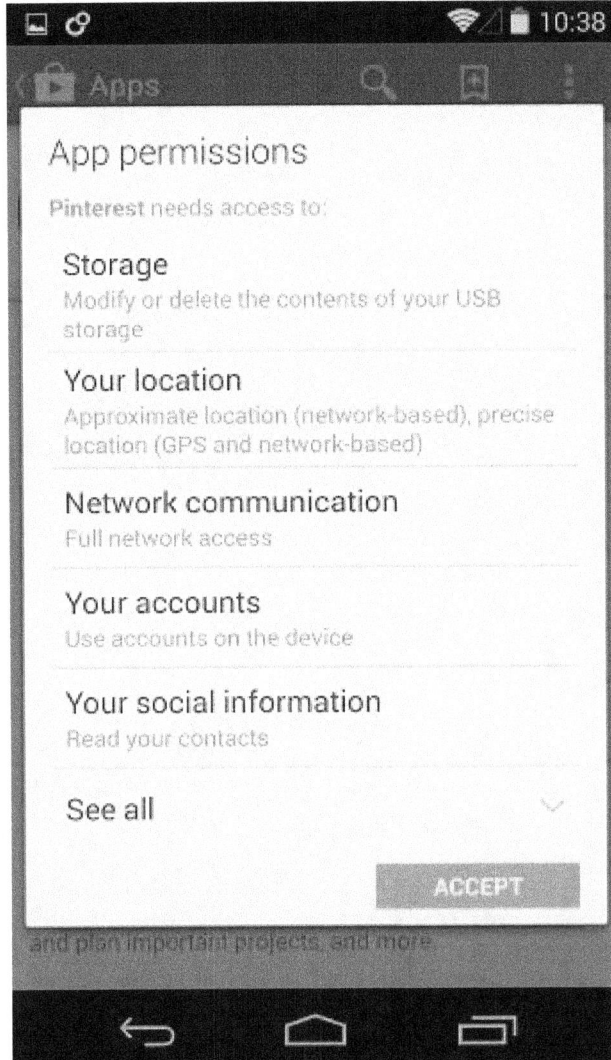

Figure 7: Permissions Screen

4. Uninstalling an Application

Within the first 15 minutes of purchasing an application, it can be uninstalled for a full refund. After 15 minutes have passed, the following instructions only apply to uninstalling an application without receiving a refund. To request a refund and uninstall an application while using the Android Market:

1. Touch the ⊞ icon at the bottom of the Home screen. The Application screen appears.
2. Touch and hold the application that you wish to uninstall. The phone briefly vibrates and 'Uninstall' appears at the top of the screen, as shown in **Figure 8**.

3. Drag the application icon over 'Uninstall', until the word turns red. Release your finger from the screen. A confirmation dialog appears. Touch **OK**. The application is uninstalled and a refund is given if less than 15 minutes have passed.

Note: Refer to "Installing a Previously Purchased Application" *to learn how to re-download an application.*

Figure 8: Uninstalling an Application

5. Closing Applications Running in the Background

Most applications will keep running even after they are exited, and some take up a considerable amount of memory. To speed up the performance of the phone, try closing some or all of these applications while they are not in use. To close an application running in the background, touch the ▭ icon at the bottom of the screen at any time. A list of recently opened applications appears, as shown in **Figure 9**. Touch an application and slide your finger to the left or right. The application is closed and disappears from the list.

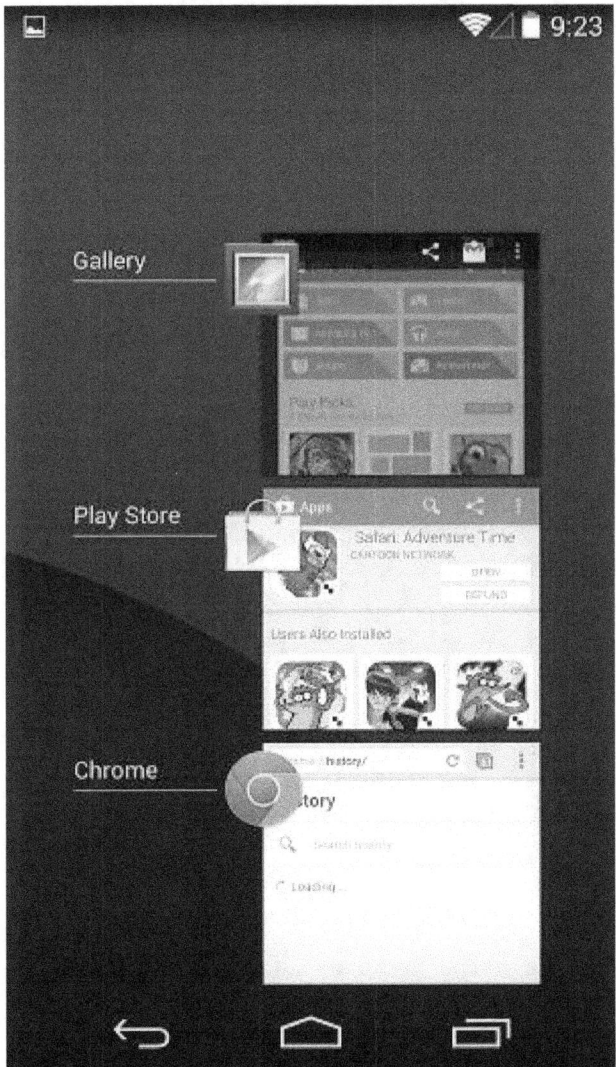

Figure 9: List of Recently Opened Applications

6. Organizing Applications into Folders

The phone can store applications in folders on the Home screens. This is especially useful to reduce clutter and to be able to find applications faster. To create a folder on the Home screen:

1. Touch and hold an application icon. The phone briefly vibrates and 'Remove' appears at the top of the screen.
2. Drag the application icon on top of another one until a white circle appears around both icons, as outlined in **Figure 10**. A folder is created.
3. Touch the new folder. The folder opens and the contained applications are shown. Touch **Unnamed folder** and enter a name for the new folder. Touch **Done** in the bottom right-hand corner of the keyboard. The folder name is saved.
4. Touch and hold an icon inside a folder and drag it anywhere outside of it. The application icon is removed from the folder. Once an application folder has only one icon remaining, the icon is placed on the Home screen and the empty folder is deleted.

Figure 10: Application Folder

7. Installing a Previously Purchased Application

After purchasing an application on an Android device registered to your account, you can download the same application for free on any Android device registered to the same account. To install previously purchased applications using the Android market:
Note: You cannot install an application free of charge if you were issued a refund for that application in the past.

Refer to "Buying an Application" *on page 115 to learn how to purchase these applications again.*

1. Touch the left edge of the screen in the Play store, and move your finger to the right. The Play Store menu appears, as shown in **Figure 11**.
2. Touch **My Apps**. The My Apps screen appears, as shown in **Figure 12**.
3. Touch **ALL** at the top of the screen. All of the applications that you have purchased or downloaded in the past appear.
4. Touch the name of the application that you wish to install. The Application description appears. Refer to *"Switching Between Google Accounts"* on page 125 to learn how to view applications purchased under a different Google account registered to your phone.
5. Touch the [INSTALL] button. The Permissions screen appears.
6. Touch the [ACCEPT] button. The application is installed on your phone.

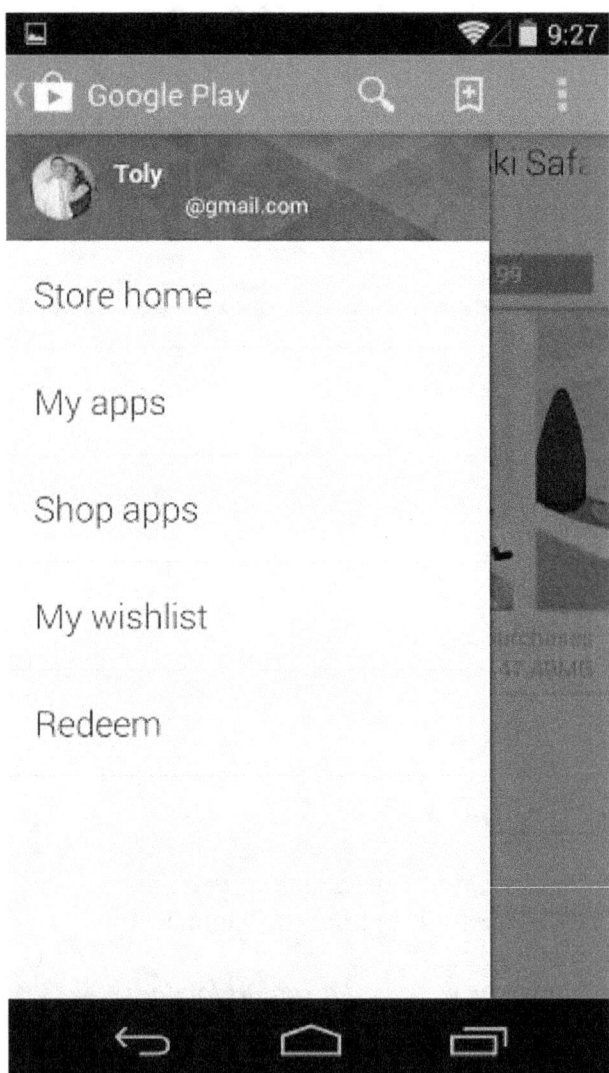

Figure 11: Play Store Menu

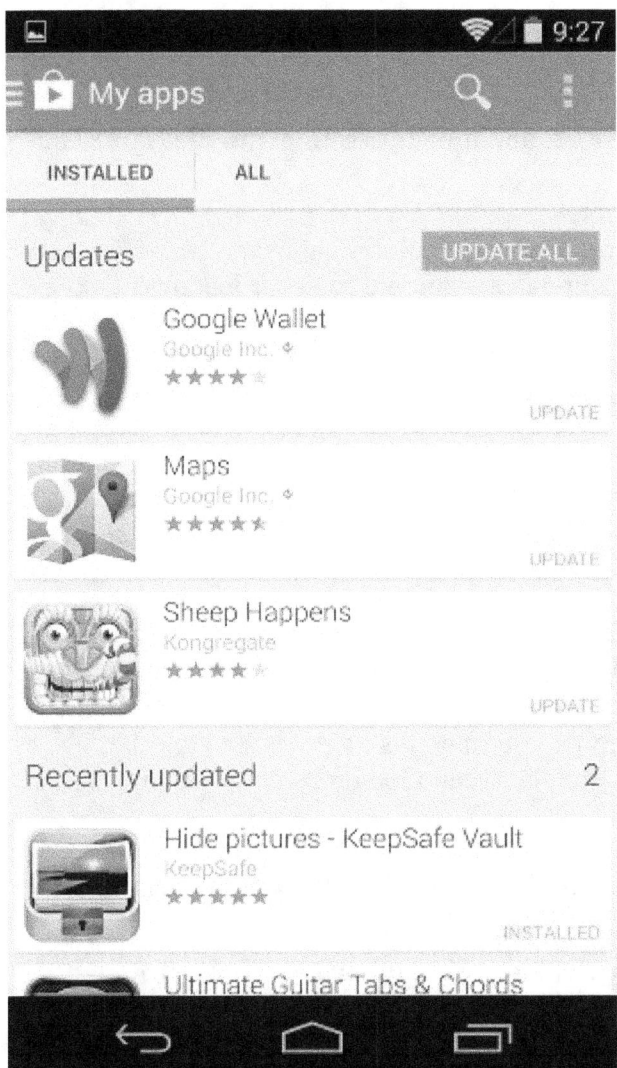

Figure 12: My Apps Screen

8. Updating Installed Applications

Application developers will sometimes release updates for their applications. To update your installed applications while using the Play Store:

1. Touch the left edge of the screen in the Play store, and move your finger to the right. The Play Store menu appears.
2. Touch **My Apps**. The My Apps screen appears.
3. Touch an application under 'Updates'. The Application description appears. If there are no applications under 'Updates', then there are no updates available for your installed applications.
4. Touch **Update**. The Permissions screen appears.
5. Touch the [ACCEPT] button. The application is updated.

*Note: You can also touch **UPDATE ALL** to the right of 'Updates' to update all applications at once.*

9. Switching Between Google Accounts

If you use more than one Google account on your phone, you may wish to switch to another account to download and manage applications. To switch between Google Accounts while using the Play Store:

1. Touch the left edge of the screen in the Play store, and move your finger to the right. The Play Store menu appears.
2. Touch the [▼] arrow to the right of your email address, as outlined in **Figure 13**.
3. Touch an account in the list. The selected account will now be used to purchase and manage applications.

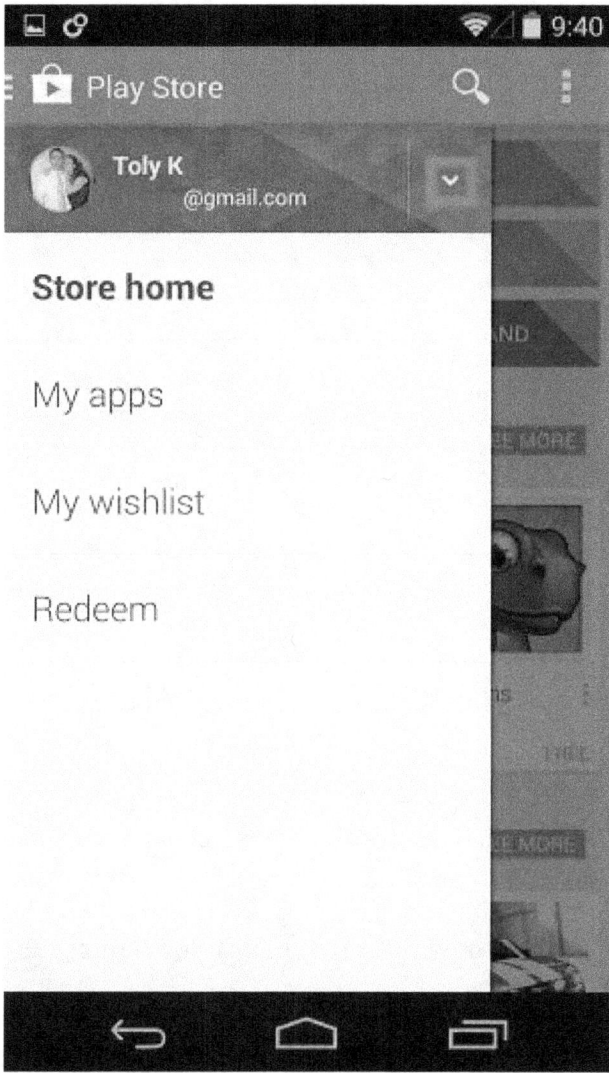

Figure 13: Switching Between Google Accounts

Adjusting Wireless Settings

Table of Contents

1. Setting Up Wi-Fi

Use a nearby Wi-Fi hotspot or a home router to avoid using your data. Wi-Fi is required to download large applications. To turn on Wi-Fi:

1. Touch the ⊞ icon at the bottom of the Home screen. The Application screen appears, as shown in **Figure 1**.

2. Touch the ⚙ icon. The Settings screen appears, as shown in **Figure 2**. If you do not see the ⚙ icon, scroll through the application screens to find it.

3. Touch **Wi-Fi**. The Wi-Fi settings screen appears.

4. Touch the OFF switch in the upper right-hand corner of the screen, if Wi-Fi is still turned off. The ON switch appears and Wi-Fi is turned on. A list of available Wi-Fi networks appears, as shown in **Figure 3**.

5. Touch the name of a Wi-Fi network. The Wi-Fi Network Password prompt appears, if the network is password protected, as shown in **Figure 4**. Otherwise, the Nexus 5 connects to the Wi-Fi network.

6. Enter the network password, if required, which is usually found on your wireless router. Touch **Connect**. The Nexus 5 connects to the Wi-Fi network.

Figure 1: Application Screen

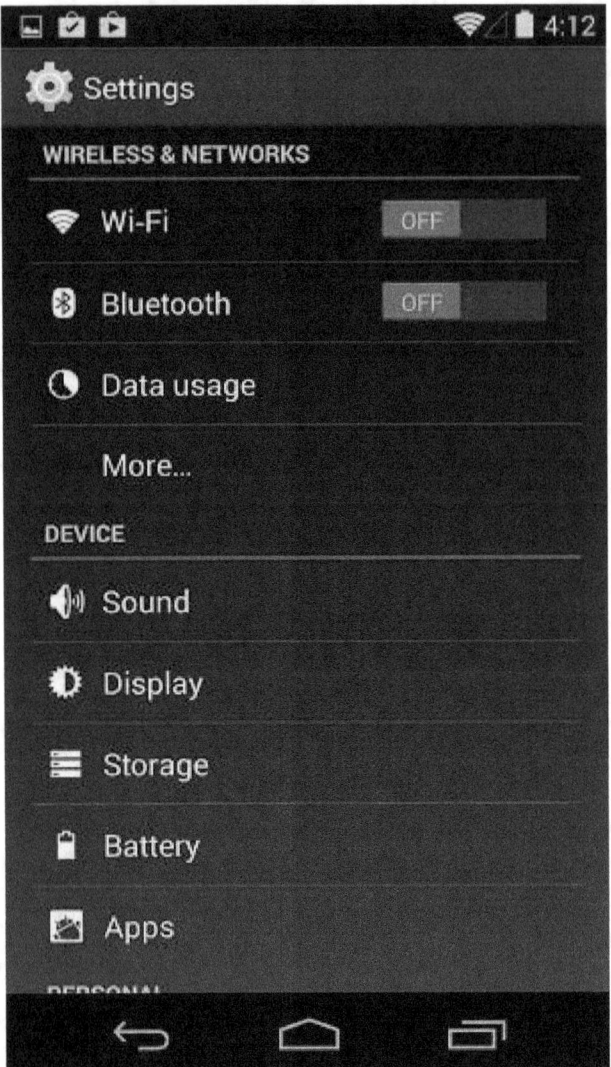

Figure 2: Settings Screen

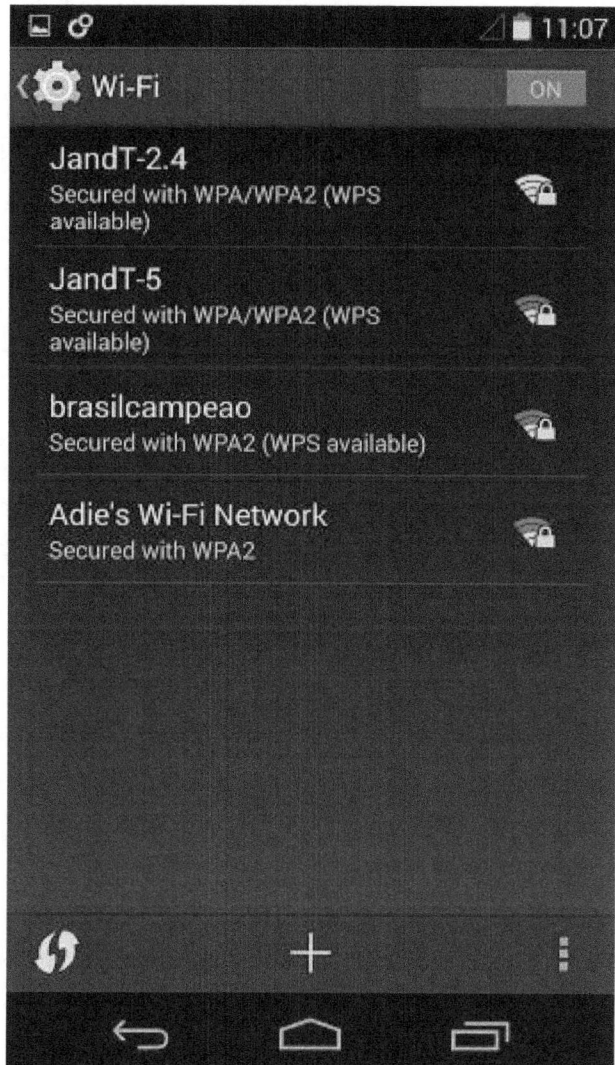

Figure 3: List of Available Wi-Fi Networks

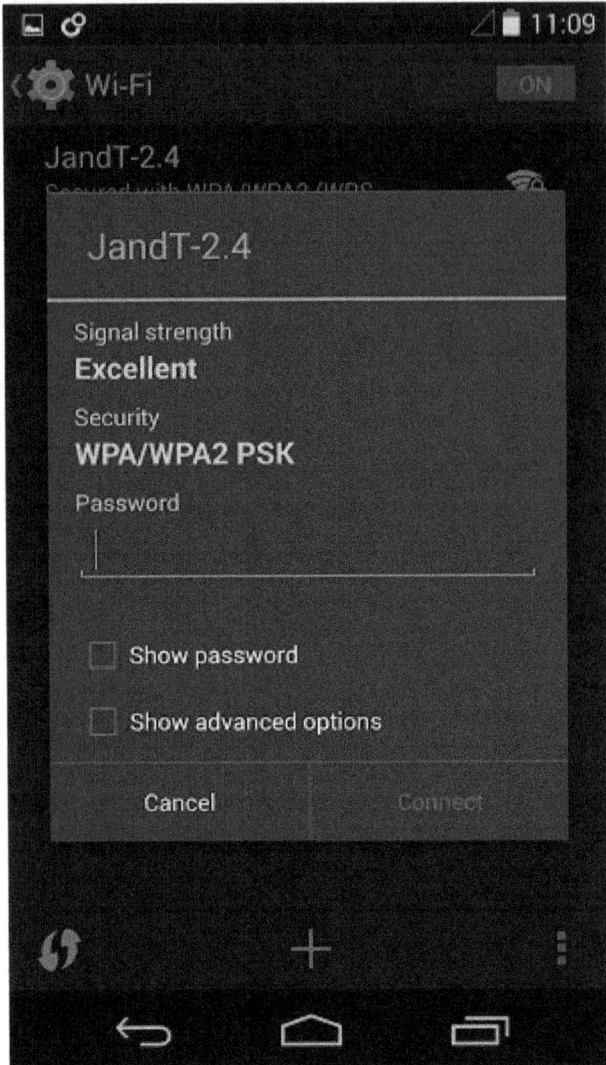

Figure 4: Network Password Prompt

2. Setting Up Bluetooth

To use a wireless Bluetooth headset or transfer media to another device without the use of Wi-Fi, you will need to turn on Bluetooth. However, if you leave it on while your headset is not in use, it may significantly reduce the battery life of your phone. To turn Bluetooth on or off:

1. Touch the ⊞ icon at the bottom of the Home screen. The Application screen appears.

2. Touch the ⚙ icon. The Settings screen appears. If you do not see the ⚙ icon, scroll through the application screens to find it.

3. Touch **Bluetooth**. The Bluetooth Settings screen appears.
4. Touch the OFF switch in the upper right-hand corner of the screen. The ON switch appears and Bluetooth is turned on. A list of Bluetooth devices that are within range and able to pair with the Nexus 5 appears, as shown in **Figure 5**. To make the Nexus 5 visible to other devices, touch **Nexus 5** at the top of the Bluetooth Settings screen. The Nexus 5 becomes visible for two minutes.
5. Touch a device in the list. The Pairing Request window appears, as shown in **Figure 6**.
6. Touch **Pair** on both devices. The devices are paired. Some devices may have you touch **OK** instead.
7. Touch the ON switch in the upper right-hand corner of the screen, if you wish to turn off Bluetooth. Bluetooth is turned off and all paired devices are disconnected.

Figure 5: List of Available Bluetooth Devices

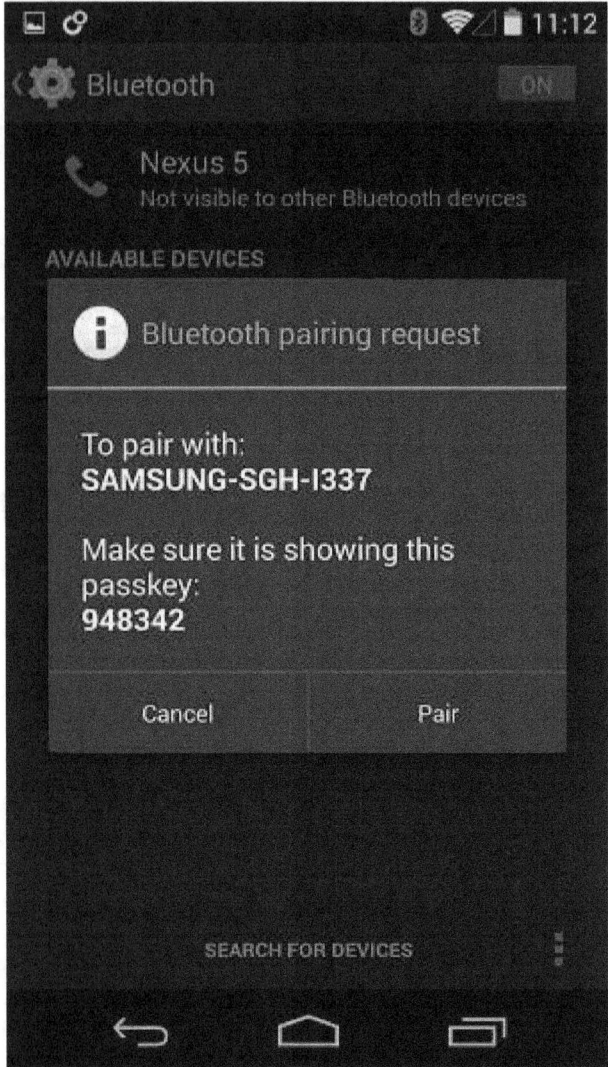

Figure 6: Pairing Request Window

3. Turning Airplane Mode On or Off

Airplanes do not allow wireless communications while in flight. Continue using your phone by enabling Airplane Mode before take-off. You may not place or receive calls, send or receive text messages or emails, or surf the Web while in Airplane Mode. Airplane Mode is also useful when traveling outside of your area of service to avoid any roaming charges and to preserve battery life. To quickly turn Airplane Mode on or off, press and hold the **Power** button. The Phone Options menu appears, as shown in **Figure 7**. Touch **Airplane mode**. Airplane mode is turned on. Repeat this process to turn Airplane mode off.

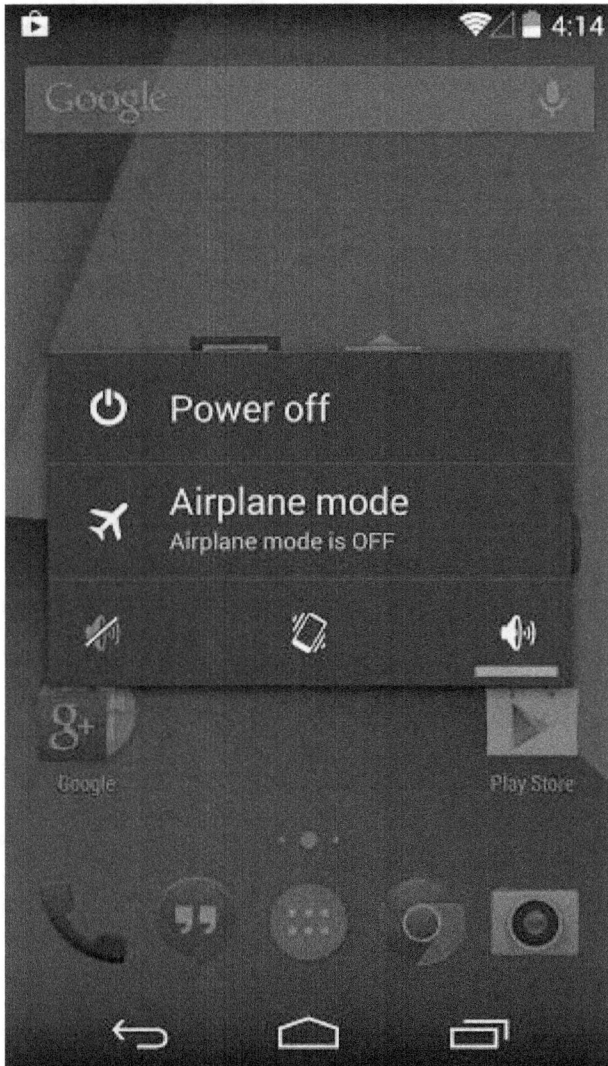

Figure 7: Phone Options Menu

4. Enabling or Disabling the Data Connection

Turning the Mobile Network on allows you to use data for email, internet, downloading applications, and using applications that require the internet. Disabling the data connection is useful when you do not have access to a Wi-Fi network and you are trying to conserve data. The data connection is turned on by default. To enable or disable the data connection:

1. Touch the ⚫ icon at the bottom of the Home screen. The Application screen appears.

2. Touch the ⚙ icon. The Settings screen appears. If you do not see the ⚙ icon, scroll through the application screens to find it.

3. Touch **More** below 'Data usage'. The Wireless Settings screen appears, as shown in **Figure 8**.

4. Touch **Mobile networks**. The Mobile Network Settings screen appears, as shown in **Figure 9**.

5. Touch **Data enabled**. The ✅ mark next to 'Data enabled' disappears and the mobile network is disabled.

6. Touch **Data enabled** again. The ✅ mark appears next to 'Data enabled' and the Mobile Network is enabled.

Note: When Wi-Fi is turned on, the data connection is automatically turned off. Only manually turn off the data connection when diagnosing a problem with spotty service.

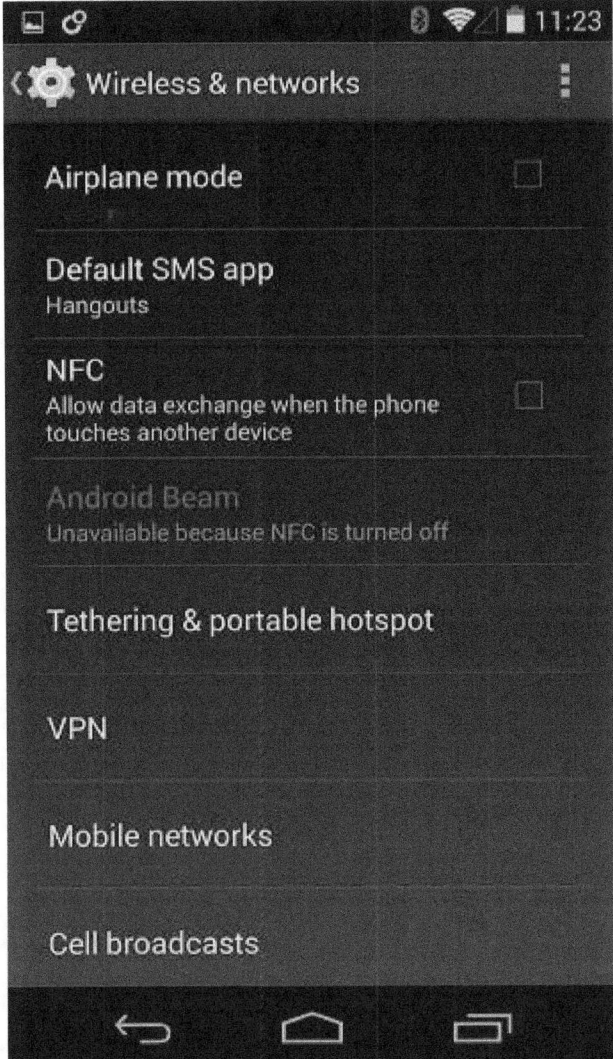

Figure 8: Wireless Settings Screen

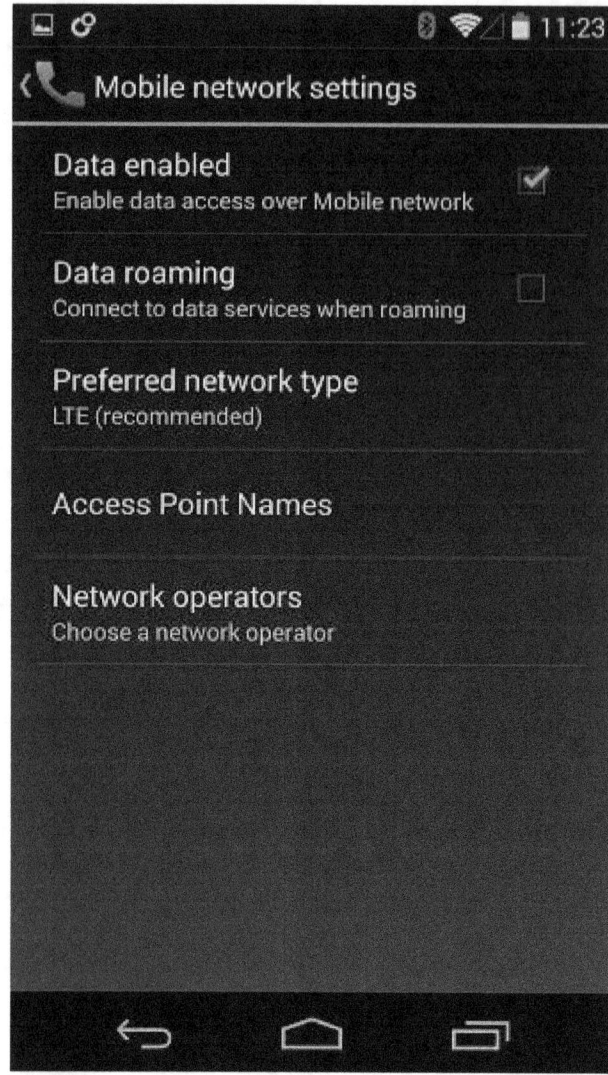

Figure 9: Mobile Network Settings Screen

5. Turning Data Roaming On or Off

When you are in an area with no wireless coverage, the Nexus 5 can use the Data Roaming feature to acquire signal from other networks. Be aware that Data Roaming can be extremely costly. Contact your network provider for details. By default, Data Roaming is turned off. To turn Data Roaming on or off:

1. Touch the ⊞ icon at the bottom of the Home screen. The Application screen appears.

2. Touch the ⚙ icon. The Settings screen appears. If you do not see the ⚙ icon, scroll through the application screens to find it.

3. Touch **More** below 'Data usage'. The Wireless Settings screen appears.
4. Touch **Mobile networks**. The Mobile Network Settings screen appears.
5. Touch **Data roaming**. A confirmation dialog appears.

6. Touch **OK**. The ✓ mark appears next to 'Data roaming' and the feature is turned on.

7. Touch **Data roaming** again. The ✓ mark next to 'Data roaming' disappears and the feature is turned off.

Adjusting Sound Settings

Table of Contents

1. Turning Vibration On or Off

The Nexus 5 can vibrate during incoming calls, notifications, and alarms. To turn vibration on or off:

1. Touch the ⊞ icon at the bottom of the Home screen. The Application screen appears, as shown in **Figure 1**.

2. Touch the ⚙ icon. The Settings screen appears, as shown in **Figure 2**. If you do not see the ⚙ icon, scroll through the application screens to find it.

3. Touch **Sound**. The Sound Settings screen appears, as shown in **Figure 3**.

4. Touch **Vibrate when ringing**. The ✓ mark appears and Vibration is turned on.

5. Touch **Vibrate when ringing** again. The ✓ mark disappears and Vibration is turned off.

Figure 1: Application Screen

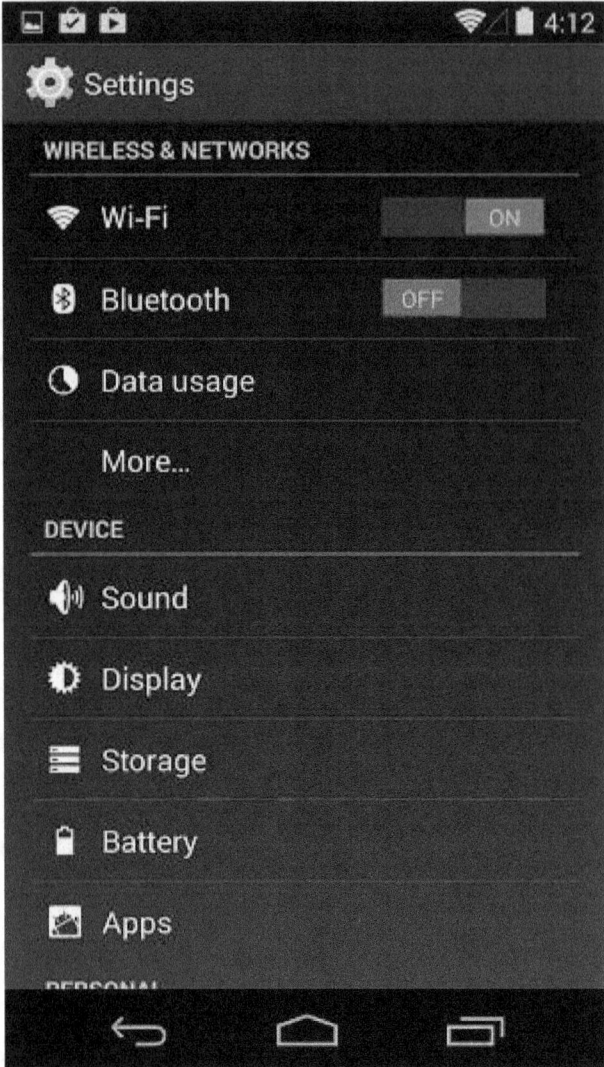

Figure 2: Settings Screen

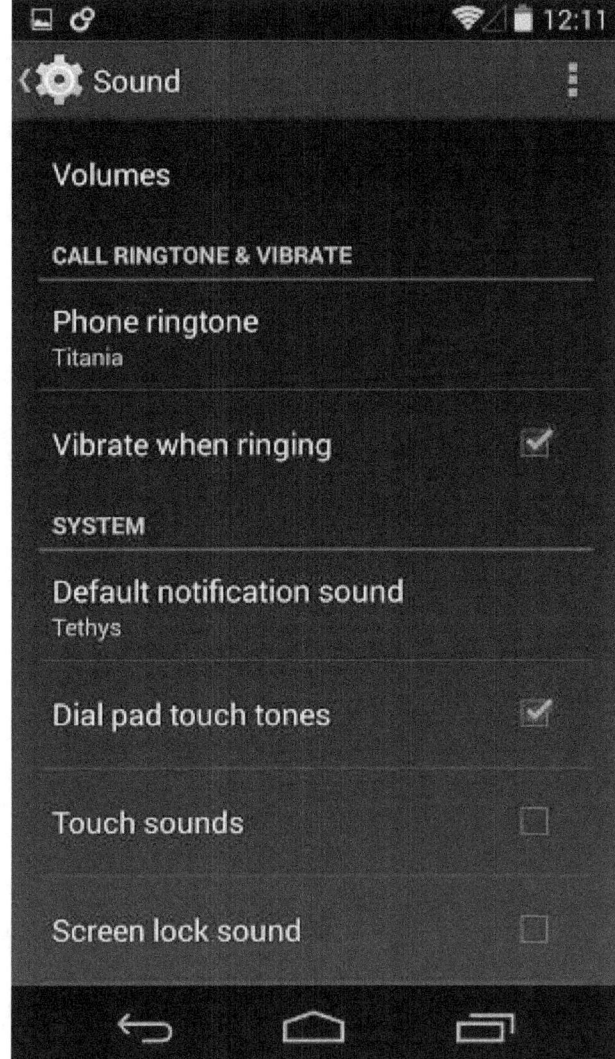

Figure 3: Sound Settings Screen

2. Setting the Ringtone, Media, and Alarm Volume

The volume for various notifications can be set separately. To set the notification volumes:

1. Touch the ⊞ icon at the bottom of the Home screen. The Application screen appears.
2. Touch the ⚙ icon. The Settings screen appears. If you do not see the ⚙ icon, scroll through the application screens to find it.
3. Touch **Sound**. The Sound Settings screen appears.
4. Touch **Volumes**. The Volume Settings window appears, as shown in **Figure 4**.

5. Touch the 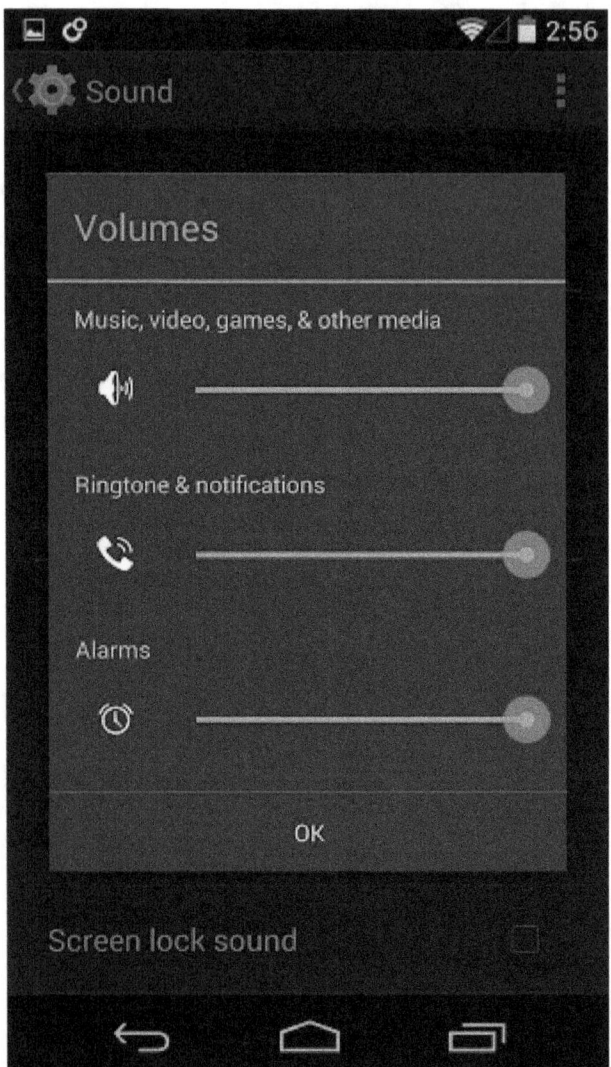 below the corresponding volume type and drag it to the left to decrease the volume or to the right to increase it. The volume is adjusted and a sound plays to preview the volume level.

6. Touch **OK**. The new volume settings are saved.

Figure 4: Volume Settings Window

3. Changing the Default Ringtone

You may change the ringtone that sounds every time somebody calls you. To set the default ringtone:

1. Touch the ⚇ icon at the bottom of the Home screen. The Application screen appears.
2. Touch the ⚙ icon. The Settings screen appears. If you do not see the ⚙ icon, scroll through the application screens to find it.
3. Touch **Sound**. The Sound Settings screen appears.
4. Touch **Phone ringtone**. A list of available ringtones appears, as shown in **Figure 5**.
5. Touch a ringtone. A preview of the entire ringtone is played.
6. Touch **OK**. The default ringtone is set.

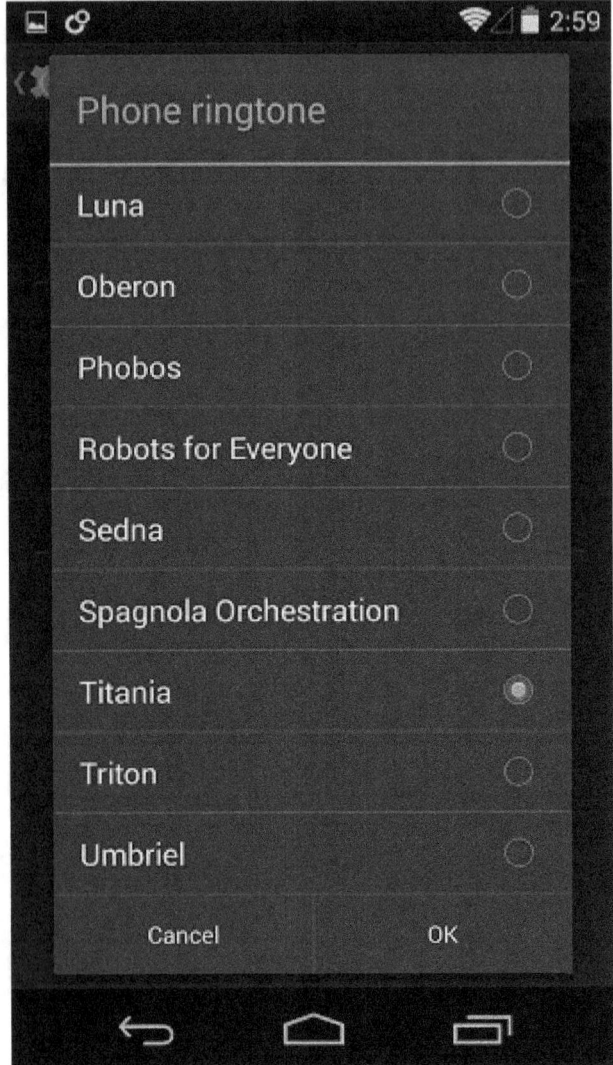

Figure 5: List of Available Ringtones

4. Changing the Default Notification Sound

When an event occurs, such as an incoming text or voicemail, a sound is played, known as the notification sound. To change the default notification sound:

1. Touch the ⊞ icon at the bottom of the Home screen. The Application screen appears.
2. Touch the ⚙ icon. The Settings screen appears. If you do not see the ⚙ icon, scroll through the application screens to find it.
3. Touch **Sound**. The Sound Settings screen appears.

4. Touch **Default notification sound**. A list of available notification sounds appears, as shown in **Figure 6**.
5. Touch a notification sound. A preview of the sound is played.
6. Touch **OK**. The default notification sound is set.

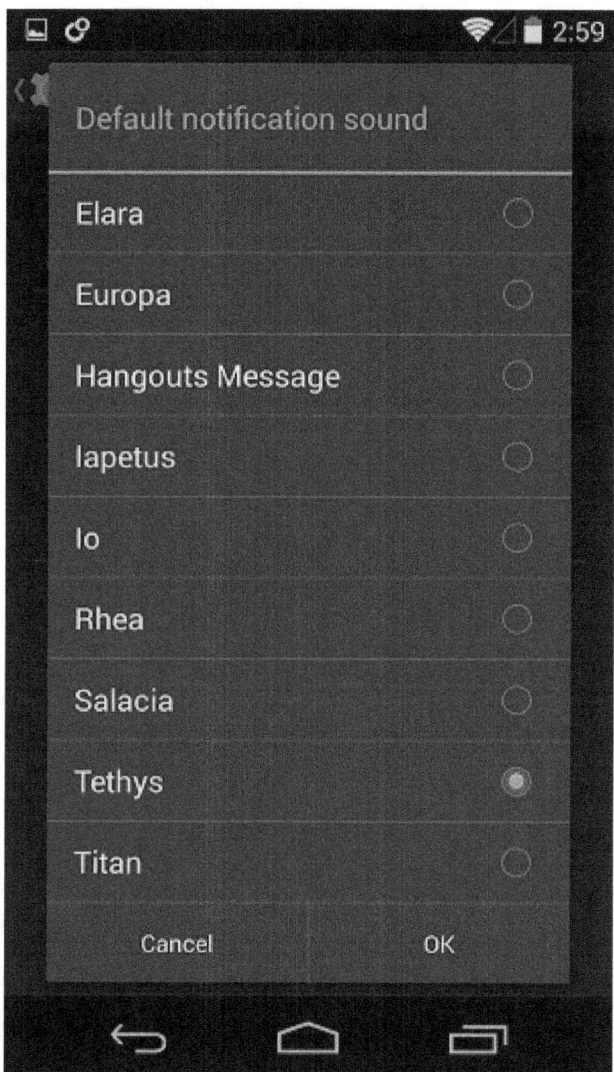

Figure 6: List of Available Notification Sounds

5. Turning System Sounds On or Off

Some system sounds, such as dial pad touch tones and screen lock sounds, can be turned on or off. To turn system sounds on or off:

1. Touch the ⊕ icon at the bottom of the Home screen. The Application screen appears.

2. Touch the ⚙ icon. The Settings screen appears. If you do not see the ⚙ icon , scroll through the application screens to find it.
3. Touch **Sound**. The Sound Settings screen appears.
4. Touch one of the following options under 'SYSTEM' to turn the corresponding sound on or off:

    -   **Dial pad touch tones** - Turns the sounds made when touching a number on the dial pad on or off.
    -   **Touch sounds** - Turns the sounds made when making a selection on the screen on or off.
    -   **Screen lock sound** - Turns the sounds made when locking and unlocking the screen on or off.
    -   **Vibrate on touch** - Turns the vibration made when making a selection on the screen on or off.

Adjusting Display Settings

Table of Contents

1. Adjusting the Brightness

The Nexus 5 can be set to automatically detect lighting conditions by using a built-in light sensor. When Automatic Brightness is turned off, a single brightness setting is maintained in any lighting. To customize the brightness settings:

1. Touch the icon at the bottom of the Home screen. The Application screen appears, as shown in **Figure 1**.

2. Touch the icon. The Settings screen appears, as shown in **Figure 2**. If you do not see the icon, scroll through the application screens to find it.

3. Touch **Display**. The Display Settings screen appears, as shown in **Figure 3**.

4. Touch **Brightness**. The Brightness window appears. By default, Automatic Brightness is turned on.

5. Touch **AUTO**. The disappears and you may now manually adjust the brightness.

6. Touch and drag the slider to the left or right. The brightness is decreased or increased, respectively.

7. Touch **OK**. The brightness is adjusted.

8. Touch **AUTO** again if you would rather have the device determine the optimal brightness. Automatic Brightness is turned on.

Figure 1: Application Screen

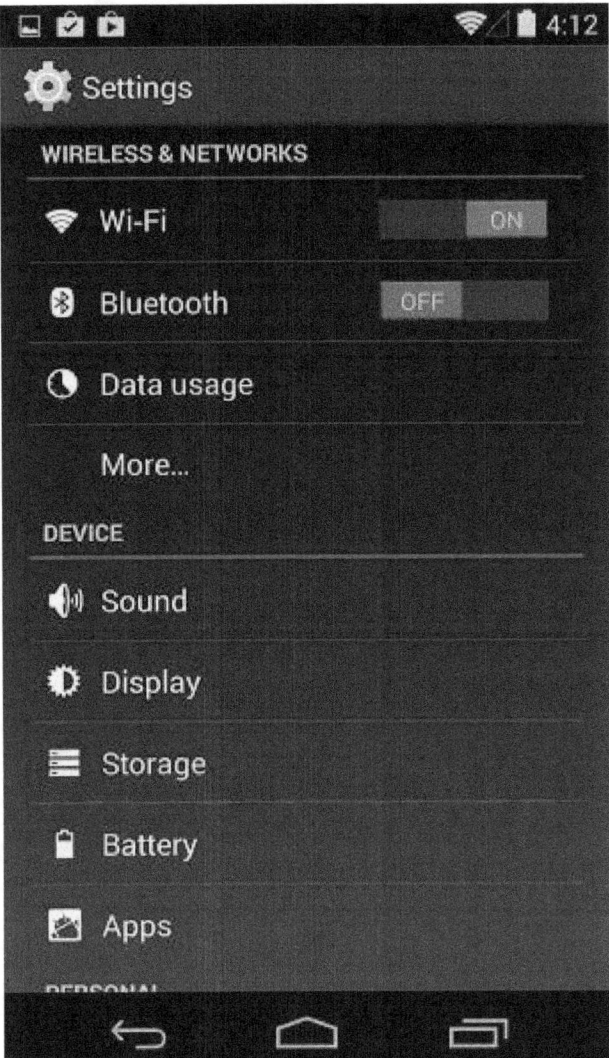

Figure 2: Settings Screen

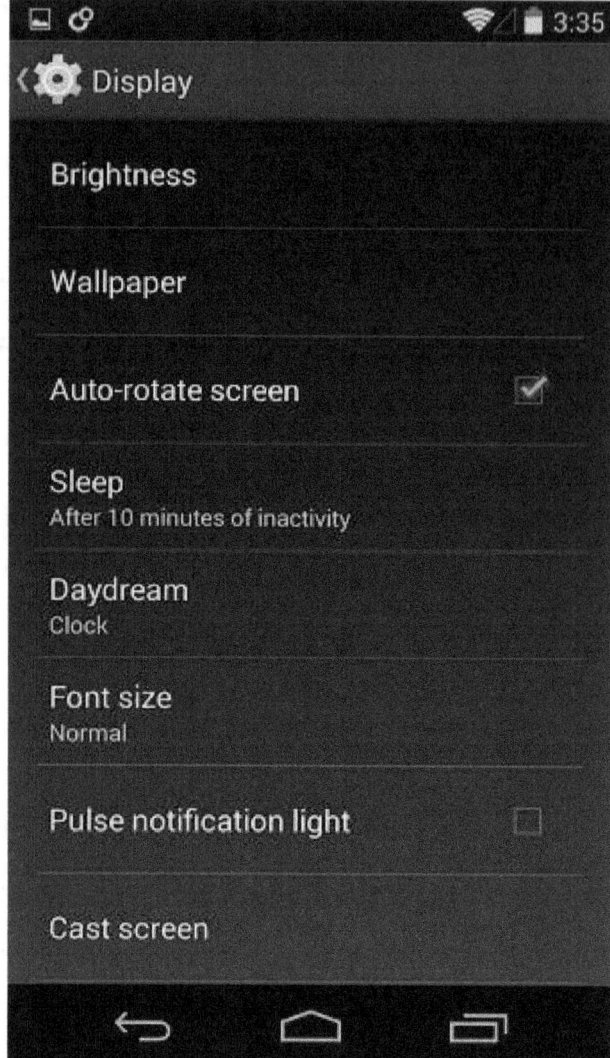

Figure 3: Display Settings Screen

2. Changing the Wallpaper

The wallpaper is the image that appears behind the application icons and widgets on the Home screens. To change the wallpaper:

1. Touch the ⊞ icon at the bottom of the Home screen. The Application screen appears.
2. Touch the ⚙ icon. The Settings screen appears. If you do not see the ⚙ icon, scroll through the application screens to find it.
3. Touch **Display**. The Display Settings screen appears.
4. Touch **Wallpaper**. The Wallpaper Source screen appears.

5. Touch **Gallery** or **Photos** to select a wallpaper from your own images, or touch one of the other options to select a pre-loaded wallpaper.

6. Touch **Set wallpaper** once you have selected an image. The wallpaper is changed to the selected image.

Note: When using an image from the Gallery, you may need to crop it first. Refer to "Editing a Photo" *on page 70 to learn how.*

3. Turning Auto-Rotate On or Off

In most applications, the screen will automatically rotate when the phone is rotated while being held upright (not laying down). By default, Auto-Rotate is turned on. To turn Auto-Rotate on or off:

1. Touch the ⬤ icon at the bottom of the Home screen. The Application screen appears.

2. Touch the ⚙ icon. The Settings screen appears. If you do not see the ⚙ icon, scroll through the application screens to find it.

3. Touch **Display**. The Display Settings screen appears.

4. Touch **Auto-rotate screen**. The ✓ mark next to 'Auto-rotate screen' disappears and the screen will no longer rotate automatically.

5. Touch **Auto-rotate screen** again. Auto-Rotate turns on and the ✓ mark reappears.

4. Changing the Sleep Timer

The Sleep Timer can be adjusted to automatically lock the Nexus 5 after it is idle for a set period of time. To change the Sleep timer:

1. Touch the ⬤ icon at the bottom of the Home screen. The Application screen appears.

2. Touch the ⚙ icon. The Settings screen appears. If you do not see the ⚙ icon, scroll through the application screens to find it.

3. Touch **Display**. The Display Settings screen appears.

4. Touch **Sleep**. The Sleep Timer settings appear, as shown in **Figure 4**.

5. Touch an option in the menu, indicating how long the phone will be idle before it locks itself. The Sleep Timer is adjusted.

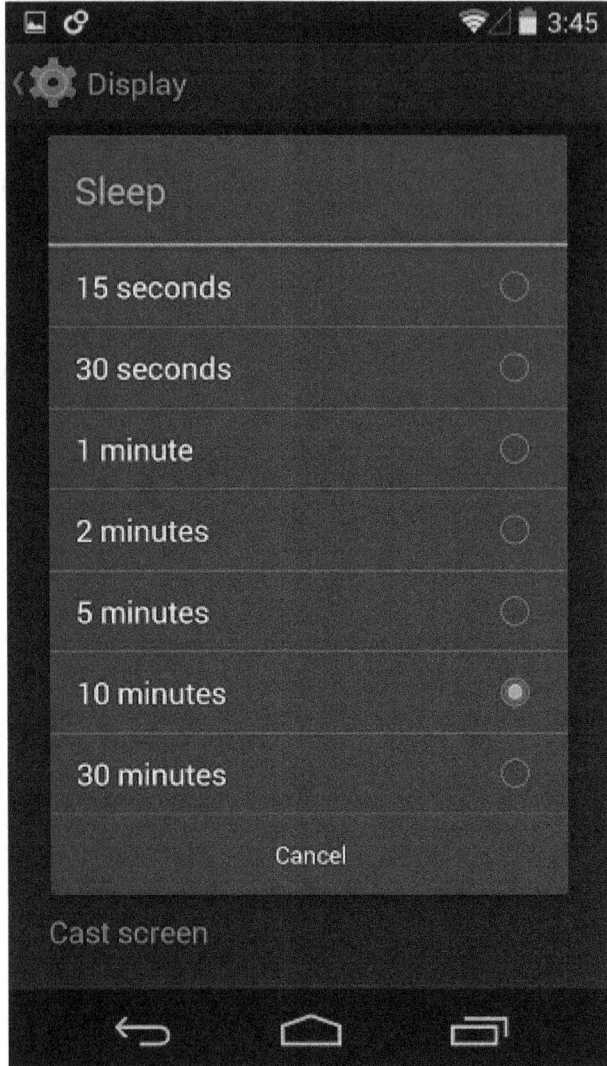

Figure 4: Sleep Timer Settings

5. Turning the Notification Light On or Off

Whenever the Nexus 5 plays a notification sound, such as for a missed call or received text, the phone can also provide a visual reminder by flashing a white LED below the screen. By default, the notification light is turned on. To turn the notification light on or off:

1. Touch the 🔲 icon at the bottom of the Home screen. The Application screen appears.

2. Touch the ⚙ icon. The Settings screen appears. If you do not see the ⚙ icon, scroll through the application screens to find it.

3. Touch **Display**. The Display Settings screen appears.

4. Touch **Pulse notification light**. The ✓ mark disappears and the notification light is turned off.

5. Touch **Pulse notification light** again. The ✓ mark reappears and the notification light is turned on.

Adjusting Security Settings

Table of Contents

1. Setting Up Screen Lock Protection

Setting a security lock can help to prevent unauthorized users from accessing your phone. There are four options for locking the screen: Face Unlock, Pattern, Personal Identification Number (PIN), and Password. To set up Screen Lock Protection:

1. Touch the ⬛ icon at the bottom of the Home screen. The Application screen appears, as shown in **Figure 1**.

2. Touch the ⚙ icon. The Settings screen appears, as shown in **Figure 2**. If you do not see the ⚙ icon, scroll through the application screens to find it.

3. Touch **Security**. The Security Settings screen appears, as shown in **Figure 3**.

4. Touch **Screen lock**. The Screen Lock options appear.

5. Touch one of the following options to learn how to set the corresponding Screen Lock:

   - **None** - No screen lock. The screen is automatically unlocked when you press the **Power** button.
   - **Slide** - The default screen lock, which requires you to touch the lock icon and slide it in any direction to unlock the screen.
   - **Face unlock** - Hold the phone at eye level, clearly showing your face. The phone recognizes facial features. This method is not fool-proof, however, as poor lighting sometimes causes the phone to stop recognizing your face. If the phone does not recognize you, you will need to draw the set pattern or enter the set PIN. On the other hand, if someone whose facial features strongly resemble yours tries to unlock the phone, it may unlock.
   - **Pattern** - Draw a pattern on the screen.

- **PIN**- Enter a series of numbers to use as a passcode.
- **Password** - Enter an alphanumeric code.

To set up a Face lock:

1. Touch **Face Unlock**. The Face Unlock screen appears.
2. Review the warnings and touch **Set it up**. The Face Lock suggestions appear.
3. Hold the phone at eye level and touch **Continue**. The phone analyzes your facial features. A check mark appears when it is finished.
4. Touch **Continue**. The Backup Lock screen appears.
5. Touch a lock you wish to use in the case that the phone does not recognize you. Draw a pattern or enter a pin, depending on your choice. You will need to enter the patter or pin twice.
6. Touch **Continue**. The Face lock is set up. To unlock your phone, press the **Power** button once and then make sure that your face is in the frame.

To set up a Pattern lock:

1. Touch **Pattern**. The Pattern screen appears.
2. Draw the desired pattern. The pattern is entered.
3. Touch **Continue**. A confirmation screen appears.
4. Draw the same pattern. The pattern is stored.
5. Touch **Confirm**. The Pattern lock is set.

To set up a PIN lock:

1. Touch **PIN**. The PIN Lock screen appears.
2. Type the desired PIN. The PIN is entered. A PIN must be between four and 16 digits in length.
3. Touch **Continue**. A confirmation screen appears.
4. Type the PIN again. The PIN is entered.
5. Touch **OK**. The PIN lock is set.

To set up a Password lock:

1. Touch **Password**. The Password screen appears.
2. Type the desired password. The password is entered. A password must be between four and 16 characters in length.
3. Touch **Continue**. A confirmation screen appears.
4. Type the same password again. The password is entered.
5. Touch **OK**. The Password lock is set.

Figure 1: Application Screen

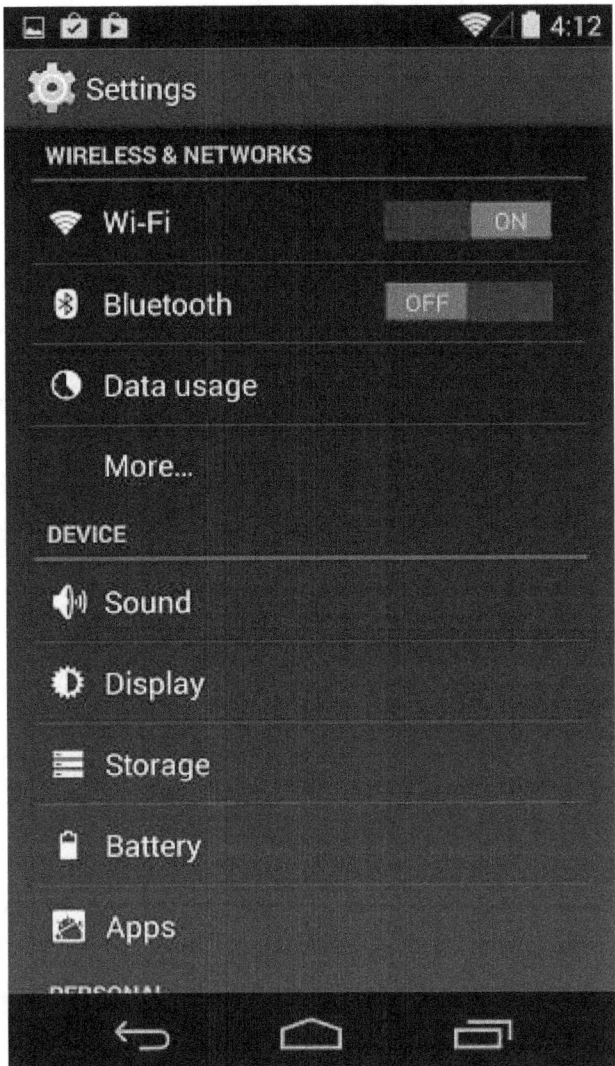

Figure 2: Settings Screen

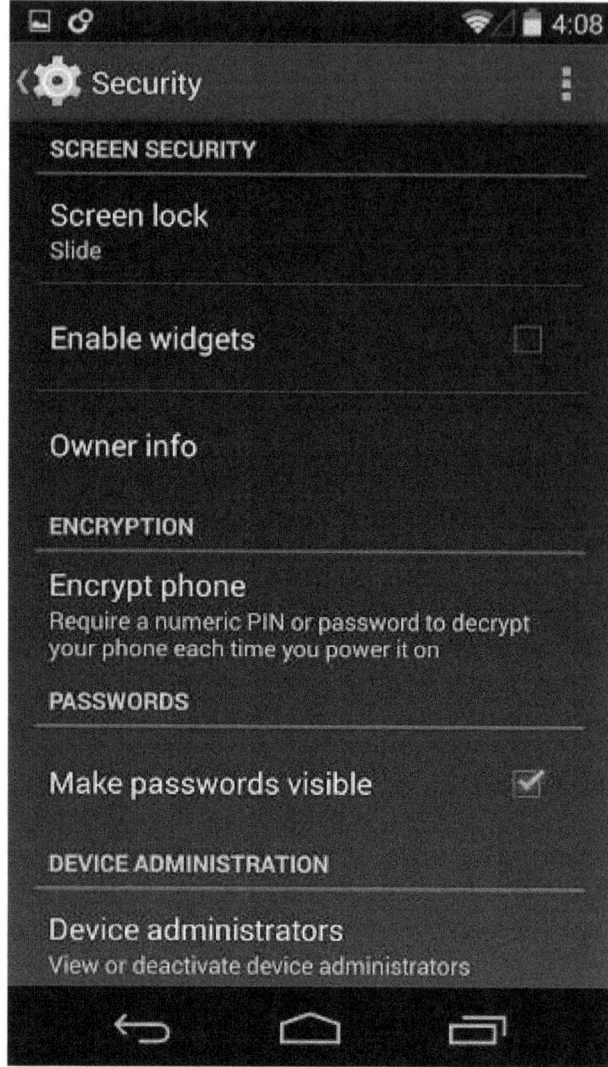

Figure 3: Security Settings

2. Changing the Automatic Lock Time

After the Nexus 5 is locked using the Power button, it will not require a password or pattern right away unless the Lock time is set to 'Immediately'. The phone may be set to wait a certain amount of time before prompting for the screen lock. To change the Lock time:

Warning: Setting the Lock time to anything but 'Immediately' will leave your phone unprotected for the set period of time.

1. Touch the ⊞ icon at the bottom of the Home screen. The Application screen appears.

2. Touch the ⚙ icon. The Settings screen appears. If you do not see the ⚙ icon, scroll through the application screens to find it.
3. Touch **Security**. The Security Settings screen appears.
4. Touch **Automatically lock**. A list of time options appears, as shown in **Figure 4**.
5. Touch an option in the menu. The lock time is set. The phone will wait the selected amount of time after being locked before requesting a screen lock.

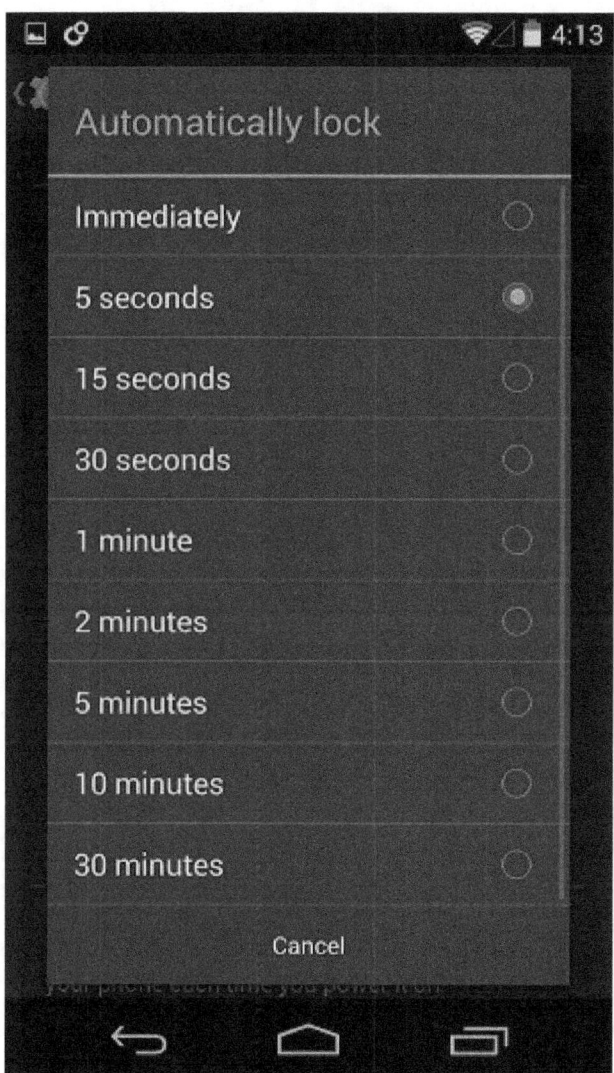

Figure 4: List of Time Options

3. Changing the Screen Lock

After setting up Screen Lock Protection, the password or pattern can be changed at any time. To change the screen lock or to turn it off:

1. Touch the ⊞ icon at the bottom of the Home screen. The Application screen appears.

2. Touch the ⚙ icon. The Settings screen appears. If you do not see the ⚙ icon, scroll through the application screens to find it.
3. Touch **Security**. The Security Settings screen appears.
4. Touch **Screen lock**. The phone asks you for your PIN, password, pattern, or face.
5. Unlock the phone using your current lock. The Screen Lock options appear.
6. Touch **None** or **Slide**. Screen lock protection is turned off. Alternatively, touch another option to set a different screen lock. Refer to *"Setting Up Screen Lock Protection"* on page 156 to learn how to set up a different type of Screen Lock Protection.

4. Making Passwords Visible

When entering a password, it can be concealed to prevent anyone from viewing it over your shoulder. However, it may be more convenient to see what is being typed. To make passwords visible:

1. Touch the ⊞ icon at the bottom of the Home screen. The Application screen appears.

2. Touch the ⚙ icon. The Settings screen appears. If you do not see the ⚙ icon, scroll through the application screens to find it.
3. Touch **Security**. The Security Settings screen appears.

4. Touch **Make passwords visible**. A ✓ mark appears next to 'Make passwords visible' and the feature is turned on.

5. Touch **Make passwords visible** again. The ✓ mark next to 'Make passwords visible' disappears and the feature is turned off.

5. Allowing the Installation of Applications from Unknown Sources

If you wish to install applications from sources other than the Android Market, you must first set the Nexus 5 to allow such installations. To allow the installation of applications from unknown sources:

1. Touch the ⬤ icon at the bottom of the Home screen. The Application screen appears.

2. Touch the ⚙ icon. The Settings screen appears. If you do not see the ⚙ icon, scroll through the application screens to find it.

3. Touch **Security**. The Security Settings screen appears.

4. Touch **Unknown sources**. A ✅ mark appears next to 'Unknown sources' and the feature is turned on.

5. Touch **Unknown sources** again. The ✅ mark next to 'Unknown sources' disappears and the feature is turned off.

Adjusting Language and Input Settings

Table of Contents

1. Changing the Phone Language

The Nexus 5 has 55 built-in languages from which to choose. Setting an alternate phone language will make all menu options and buttons appear in the selected language. Web pages and other content will still be displayed in the language in which they were originally written. To change the phone language:

1. Touch the ⬛ icon at the bottom of the Home screen. The Application screen appears, as shown in **Figure 1**.

2. Touch the ⚙ icon. The Settings screen appears, as shown in **Figure 2**. If you do not see the ⚙ icon, scroll through the application screens to find it.

3. Scroll down and touch **Language & input**. The Language & Input Settings screen appears, as shown in **Figure 3**.

4. Touch **Language**. A list of available languages appears, as shown in **Figure 4**.

5. Touch a language. The phone's language is changed to the selected option.

Figure 1: Application Screen

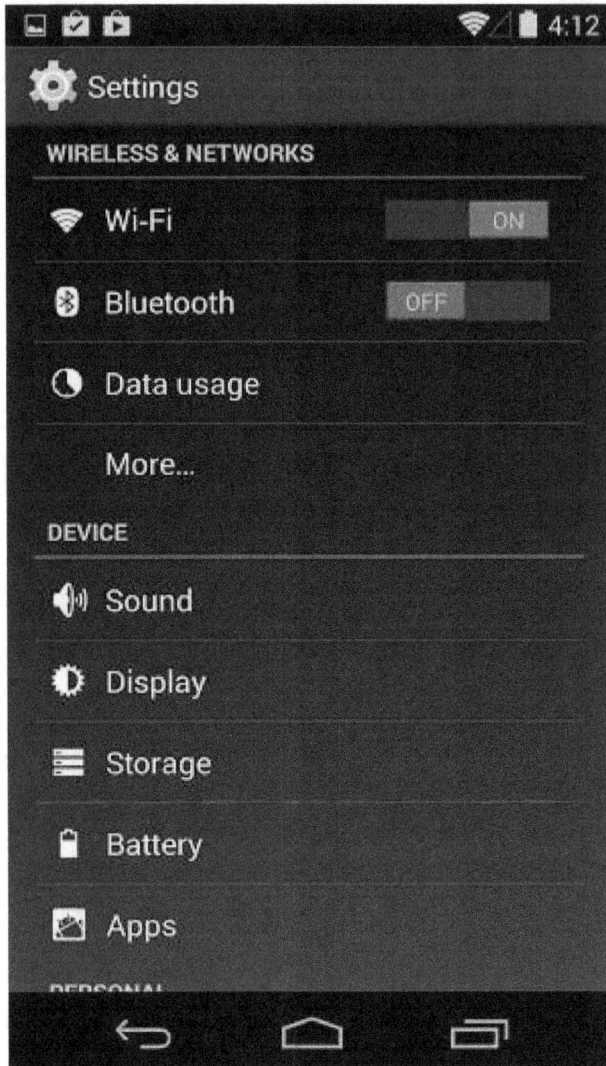

Figure 2: Settings Screen

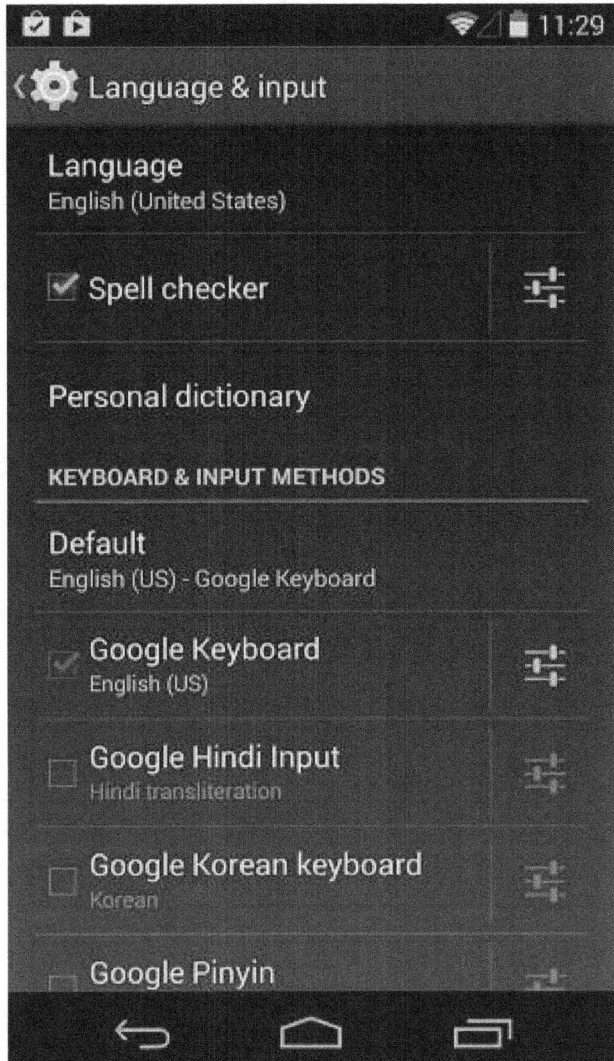

Figure 3: Language and Input Settings Screen

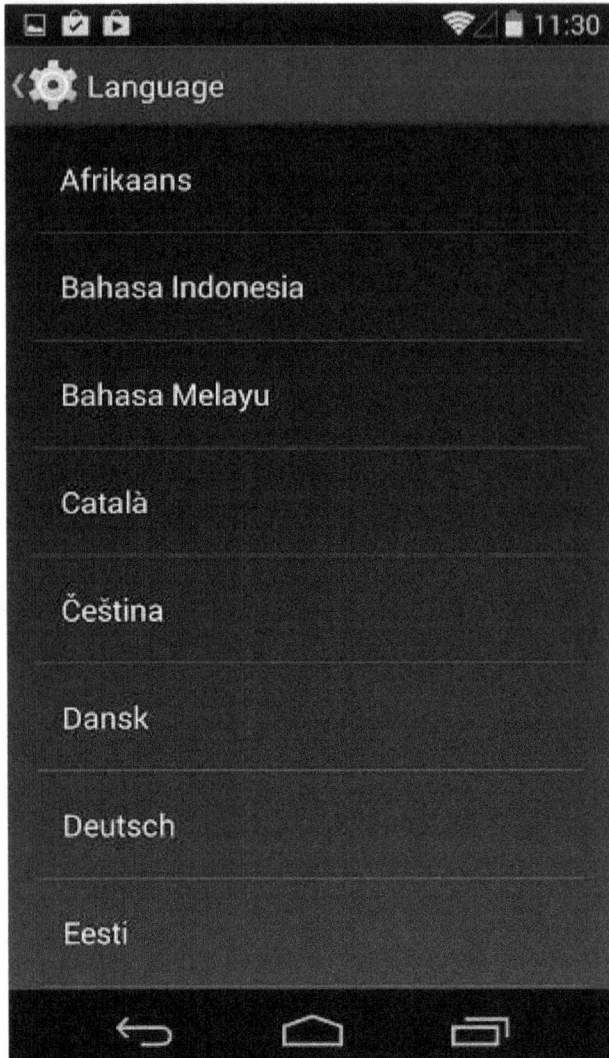

Figure 4: List of Available Languages

2. Turning Spelling Correction On or Off

The Nexus 5 can notify you when you have misspelled a word by underlining it with a red line. You can then touch the word and touch a suggestion from a list to replace the original word. By default, Spelling Correction is turned on. To turn Spelling Correction on or off:

1. Touch the ⊞ icon at the bottom of the Home screen. The Application screen appears.

2. Touch the ⚙ icon. The Settings screen appears. If you do not see the ⚙ icon, scroll through the application screens to find it.

3. Touch **Language & input**. The Language & Input Settings screen appears.

4. Touch **Spelling checker**. A ✓ mark appears next to 'Spelling correction' and the feature is turned on.

5. Touch **Spelling checker** again. The ✓ mark next to 'Spelling correction' disappears and the feature is turned off.

3. Adding Words to the Personal Dictionary

The Nexus 5 can store custom words in the Personal Dictionary in order to improve suggestions while you type. Words added to the personal dictionary will not be detected as misspelled ones. In addition, you may add shortcuts, such as "BRB" (for Be Right Back), that will automatically expand when typed. For instance, if you add "TTYL" and enter "Talk to You Later" in the 'Shortcut' field (see step 6 below), and then enter it in a text or email, the phone will automatically replace "TTYL" with "Talk to You Later." To add words to the Personal Dictionary:

1. Touch the ⊞ icon at the bottom of the Home screen. The Application screen appears.

2. Touch the ⚙ icon. The Settings screen appears. If you do not see the ⚙ icon, scroll through the application screens to find it.

3. Touch **Language & input**. The Language & Input Settings screen appears.

4. Touch **Personal dictionary**. The Personal Dictionary screen appears, as shown in **Figure 5**.

5. Touch the ➕ icon in the upper right-hand corner of the screen. The Add to Dictionary window appears.

6. Enter the word that you wish to add and touch **OK**. The word is added to your Personal Dictionary. You may also enter a shortcut in the 'Shortcut' field.

Figure 5: Personal Dictionary Screen

4. Changing Android Keyboard Settings

The Android Keyboard on the Nexus 5 can be customized by editing settings like Auto-Capitalization and key press vibrations. To change the Android Keyboard settings:

1. Touch the ⊞ icon at the bottom of the Home screen. The Application screen appears.
2. Touch the ⚙ icon. The Settings screen appears. If you do not see the ⚙ icon, scroll through the application screens to find it
3. Touch **Language & input**. The Language & Input Settings screen appears.

4. Touch the [icon] icon next to 'Google keyboard'. The Android Keyboard Settings screen appears, as shown in **Figure 6**.
5. Touch one of the following options to customize it:

Note: A [checkmark] *mark indicates that one of the features described above is turned on.*

- **Auto-capitalization** - Automatically capitalizes the first word of every sentence.
- **Vibrate on keypress** - Vibrates every time a key is touched on the keyboard.
- **Sound on keypress** - Makes a clicking sound every time a key is touched on the keyboard.
- **Popup on keypress -** Magnifies the letter every time a key is touched on the keyboard.

- **Show settings key** - Shows the [icon] key below the 'z' key on the keyboard. Touch the [icon] key at any time to customize Keyboard settings.

- **Voice input key** - Customizes the location of the [icon] key on the keyboard. If you choose the 'Symbols keyboard' option, touch the [?123 icon] on the keyboard to find the [icon] key. Turn off this feature to remove the [icon] key from the keyboard.

- **Add-on dictionaries** - Displays a list of additional dictionaries that can be used for text suggestions. If a dictionary is not 'Installed', touch the dictionary to install it.
- **Auto-correction** - Sets the level of automatic correction, from 'Modest' to 'Very aggressive'. Choosing the 'Very aggressive' option will make the phone auto correct almost every misspelled word. Selecting 'Off' will turn off automatic correction.
- **Show correction suggestions** - Customizes when correction suggestions are shown, either always, only in portrait mode, or never.
- **Enable gesture typing** - Allows you to type a word by touching the first word, then sliding your finger to each subsequent letter, and removing your finger from the screen once you have reached the final letter.
- **Dynamic floating preview** - Suggests the closest matching word while you are using gesture typing.
- **Show gesture trail -** Shows the trail that your finger follows while you are using gesture typing.
- **Phrase gesture** - Allows you to enter entire phrases, including spaces between words, by sliding your finger to the space bar after each word. When using this feature, you do not have to lift your finger off of the screen in order to type an entire sentence.

- **Next-word suggestions** - Suggests the word that will most likely come next in the sentence based on the word that you have just entered.

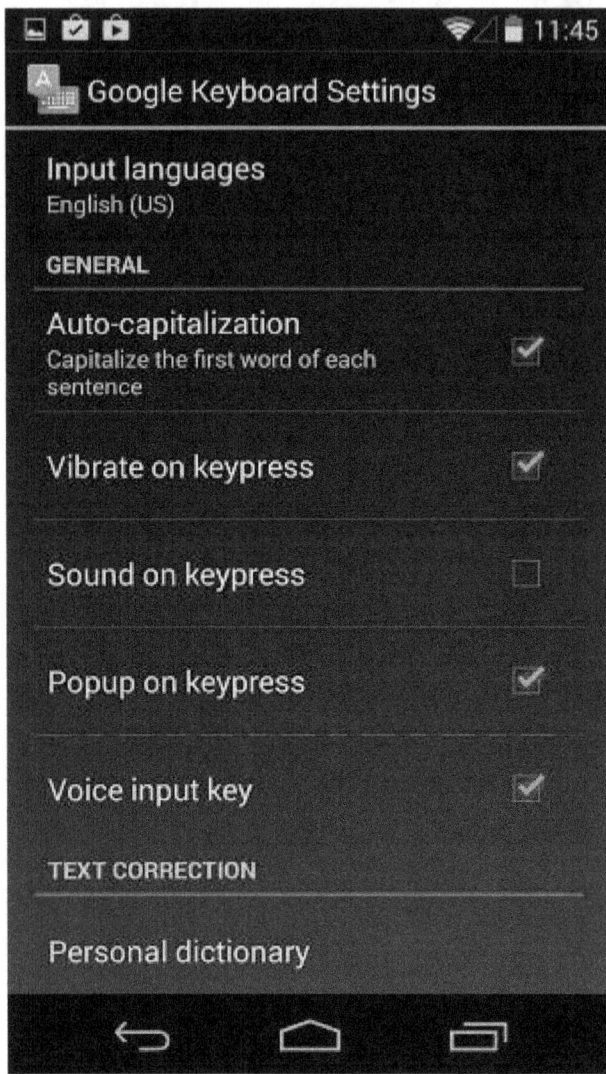

Figure 6: Google Keyboard Settings Screen

5. Changing Voice Search Settings

You can search the phone and the web using voice recognition by touching the 🎤 icon at the top of the Home screen. To change Voice Search settings:

1. Touch the ⊞ icon at the bottom of the Home screen. The Application screen appears.

2. Touch the ⚙ icon. The Settings screen appears. If you do not see the ⚙ icon, scroll through the application screens to find it.

3. Touch **Language & input**. The Language & Input Settings screen appears.

4. Scroll down and touch **Voice Search**. The Voice Search Settings screen appears, as shown in **Figure 7**.

5. Touch one of the following options to change it:

   - **Language -** Selects the language used by the voice recognition software. Touch the language in the list that appears.
   - **Speech output -** Turns voice responses on or off. You may also turn 'Hands-free only' mode on, which only uses voice responses when using a Bluetooth headset.
   - **Block offensive words -** Prevents the voice recognition software from entering recognized offensive words.
   - **Hotword detection -** Allows you to say "OK Google" to start a voice search.
   - **Offline speech recognition -** Allows you to install additional languages that can be used with Voice Search.
   - **Bluetooth headset -** Allows you to perform voice searches using your Bluetooth headset.

Note: A ✓ *mark indicates that the 'Block offensive words' or 'Personalized recognition' feature described above is turned on.*

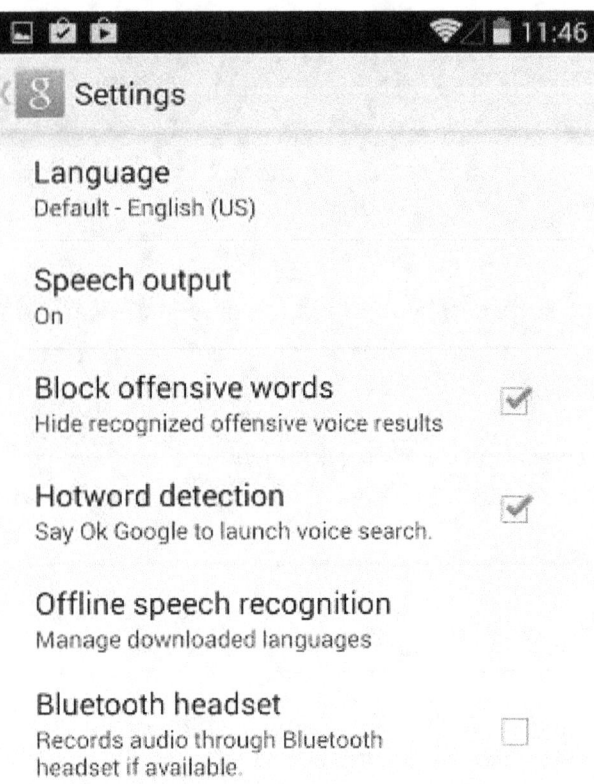

Figure 7: Voice Search Settings Screen

Tips and Tricks

Table of Contents

1. Maximizing Battery Life

There are several things you can do to increase the battery life of the Nexus 5:

- Lock the phone whenever it is not in use. To lock the phone, press the **Power** button once.
- Keep the Sleep Timer set to a small amount of time. This will dim and turn off the screen when the phone is idle. Refer to *"Changing the Sleep Timer"* on page 152 to learn how to adjust the Sleep Timer.
- Turn down the brightness or turn on Auto-Brightness. To learn how to adjust the brightness, click *"Adjusting the Brightness"* on page 148.
- Turn on Airplane Mode to turn off wireless communications. To turn on Airplane Mode, press and hold the **Power** button and then touch **Airplane mode**.

- Turn off Wi-Fi, Bluetooth, and the data connection when not in use. Only turn off the data connection when in an area with very little or no service. Refer to *"Setting Up Wi-Fi"* on page 127 to learn how to turn Wi-Fi off. Refer to *"Setting Up Bluetooth"* on page 131 to learn how to turn off Bluetooth. To learn how to turn off the data connection, refer to *"Enabling or Disabling the Data Connection"* on page 135.
- Minimize your use of the internet. Using data significantly decreases the battery life.
- Avoid using the camera and do not use the camera flash, if possible. Both need a lot of battery power to operate.

2. Adding an Extension to a Contact's Number

When entering a number for a stored contact, you may also add an extension that will be dialed following a two-second pause after the number is dialed. To add an extension, add several commas (found by touching the ⬛ * # key on the keypad) after the number. Add the extension following the commas. There is no limit to the number of commas that may be added.

Please note that the trick is to add more than one comma because most numbers will not be connected immediately. Each comma provides a one-second pause. Try dialing a number first and waiting to see how many times it rings, if any, before the machine picks up. There are exceptions, such as adding a comma and the voicemail password following *86 because voicemail is connected without ringing a single time.

3. Checking the Amount of Available Memory

To check the amount of available memory on your phone and external SD card, if one is inserted:

1. Touch the ⬛ icon at the bottom of the Home screen. The Application screen appears.

2. Touch the ⚙ icon. The Settings screen appears. If you do not see the ⚙ icon, scroll through the application screens to find it.

3. Touch **Storage**. The Internal Storage screen appears. The amount of available memory appears at the bottom of the screen.

4. Freeing Up Memory

There are several ways to free up some memory on the Nexus 5. Try one of the following tricks:

- Uninstall applications that are no longer needed. Refer to *"Uninstalling an Application"* on page 118 to learn how.
- Remove all temporary internet files. Refer to *"Clearing Personal Data"* on page 87 to learn how.

5. Viewing the Full Horizontal Keyboard

The full horizontal keyboard provides much better accuracy than the vertical keyboard. Rotate the phone onto either side while typing a text message to turn on the horizontal keyboard. Make sure that Automatic Rotation is turned on. Refer to *"Turning Auto-Rotate On or Off"* on page 152 to learn how.

6. Calling a Number from a Website

A phone number can be dialed directly from a website. Most phone numbers that can be dialed are displayed in a blue box, although this also works for those that do not formally appear in blue.

Touch the phone number. The keypad appears and the number is entered. Touch the button at the bottom of the screen. The phone dials the number.

7. Deleting a Voicemail without Listening to It

To delete a voicemail without listening to the whole thing, press **7** while it is playing. The voicemail is deleted and the next message starts to play.

8. Typing Alternate Characters

While typing a sentence, insert other letters, such as Á or Ñ, by touching and holding the base letter. For a letter like Ñ, the base letter is the letter N. A menu of characters appears above the letter. Slide your finger to a character to insert it. The highlighted letter is inserted.

9. Using MP3's as Ringtones

Download the Winamp application to set a song from your Music library as the phone's default ringtone. Refer to *"Buying an Application"* on page 115 to learn how to install Winamp. To use MP3's as ringtones:

1. Touch the icon. The Winamp Home screen appears.
2. Touch **Songs**. A list of all songs stored on your Nexus 5 appears.
3. Touch and hold a song. The Song menu appears.
4. Touch **Use as phone ringtone**. The entire song is set as the default ringtone.

10. Muting an Email Sender

You may block an email sender using the Mute feature. To mute an email sender:

1. Touch the icon at the bottom of the Home screen. The Application screen appears.

2. Touch the icon. The Gmail application opens and the Inbox appears.
   Touch and hold an email. The email is selected.

3. Touch the icon in the upper right-hand corner of the screen. The Email settings appear.
4. Touch **Mute**. The sender is muted and the email is sent to the Trash folder. All future email from the sender will be sent directly to the 'Trash' folder.

11. Reporting Spam in the Gmail Application

When you receive an unwanted email, you can immediately mark it as spam to avoid receiving similar solicitations in the future. To report spam in the Gmail application:

1. Touch the icon at the bottom of the Home screen. The Application screen appears.

2. Touch the icon. The Gmail application opens and the Inbox appears.
3. Touch and hold an email. The email is selected.

4. Touch the icon in the upper right-hand corner of the screen. The Email settings appear.

5. Touch **Report spam**. The email is marked as spam and sent to the 'Spam' folder. All future emails from the same email address will end up in the 'Spam' folder.

12. Marking an Email as 'Unread'

If you accidentally open an email, but have no time to read it, you can mark it as 'Unread' to remind yourself to read it later. To mark an email as 'Unread':

1. Touch the ⊞ icon at the bottom of the Home screen. The Application screen appears.

2. Touch the M icon. The Gmail application opens and the Inbox appears.
3. Touch and hold an email. The email is selected.
4. Touch the ✉ icon at the top of the screen. The email is marked as 'Unread'.

13. Turning on the Camera from the Lock Screen

To turn on the camera without unlocking your phone, touch the 📷 icon on the lock screen and slide it to the left. The camera turns on.

14. Taking Panoramic Photos

The Nexus 5 allows you to take panoramic photos. To take a panoramic photo:

1. Touch the ⭘ icon. The camera turns on.
2. Touch the 📷 icon. The Camera Type menu appears.
3. Touch the ◠ icon. Panorama mode is enabled.
4. Touch the ⬤ button. The camera begins to capture the panorama.
5. Move the camera slowly from one side of the panorama to the other. Touch the ◻ button to stop capturing early. The panorama is captured and stored in the 'Camera' album in the Gallery.

15. Capturing a Screenshot without Connecting the Phone to a Computer

To capture a screenshot, press the **Power** button and **Volume Down** button at exactly the same time. Hold the buttons for two seconds. A framed picture of the current screen briefly appears and a screenshot is captured. Release the buttons. The screenshot can be found in the 'Screenshot' album in the Gallery.

16. Accessing the Phone Settings Quickly

You do not have to go through the Application screen to open the Phone settings. Touch the Notification bar at the top of the screen and slide your finger down. The Notifications appear.

Touch the icon, and then touch the icon. The Settings screen appears.

17. Clearing a Single Notification

While viewing notifications on the Notification screen (opened by touching the status bar and sliding your finger down), you can clear one notification at a time. Touch the notification and slide your finger to the left or right. The notification is cleared.

18. Taking a Picture while Shooting a Video

While capturing a video, you can take a picture without interrupting the recording. To take a picture, touch the screen anywhere. The frame briefly turns red and a picture is captured. The picture is stored in the Camera album in the Gallery, while the phone continues to record the video.

19. Calling a Nearby Location

The Nexus 5 allows you to find and instantly call local businesses and other facilities. Touch

the ☏ icon at the bottom of the screen to bring up the keypad. Then, touch **Search contacts & nearby places** at the top of the screen. Enter the name of the location that you would like to call. Matching search results appear as you type.

20. Sending All Calls from a Specific Contact to Voicemail

You may reject all calls from a specific contact by sending them directly to voicemail. To reject all calls from a contact:

1. Open the contact's information. Refer to *"Editing Contact Information"* on page 35 to learn how.

2. Touch the ⋮ icon in the upper right-hand corner of the screen. The Contact Information menu appears.

3. Touch **All calls to voicemail**. The ✓ icon appears, and all calls from the selected contact will be sent directly to voicemail.

4. Touch **All calls to voicemail** again. The ✓ icon disappears, and calls from the selected contact will come through regularly.

Troubleshooting

Table of Contents

1. Nexus 5 does not turn on

If the Nexus 5 does not turn on:

- **Recharge the phone** - Use the included wall charger to charge the battery. If the battery power is extremely low, the screen will not turn on for several minutes. Do NOT attempt to use the USB port on your computer to charge the phone, as it will not work.
- **Perform a Soft Reset** - If you have done one or both of the above and the phone still does not start, a soft reset should be performed. To perform a soft reset:

  1. Press and hold the **Power** button and touch **Power off**. The phone turns off.
  2. Wait ten seconds. Press and hold the **Power** button for three seconds. The phone turns on.

2. Nexus 5 is not responding

If the phone is frozen or is not responding, try one or more of the following. These steps typically solve most problems on the phone:

- **Restart the phone** - If the phone freezes while running an application, try holding down the **Power** button. If this does not work, the best course of action is to perform a soft reset. Refer to *"Perform a Soft Reset"* on page 182 to learn how.
- **Remove Media** - Some downloaded applications or music may freeze up the phone. After restarting the phone, try deleting some of the media. To learn how to delete an application, refer to *"Uninstalling an Application"* on page 118. You may also erase all data at once and reset your phone to factory defaults by doing the following:

Warning: Any erased data is not recoverable.

1. Touch the ⊞ icon at the bottom of the Home screen. The Application screen appears.
2. Touch the ⚙ icon. The Settings screen appears.
3. Touch **Backup & reset**. The Backup & Reset screen appears.
4. Touch **Factory Data Reset**. The Reset screen appears.
5. Touch **Reset phone**. A confirmation dialog appears.
6. Touch **Erase everything**. All data is erased and the phone resets.

3. Can't make a call

If you cannot make a call using the phone, check the following:

- **Service** - If there are no bars shown at the top right of the screen, then the network does not cover you in your location. Try walking to a different location, or even to a different part of a building.
- **Airplane Mode** - Make sure Airplane Mode is turned off. If it is already off, try turning Airplane mode on for 15 seconds and then turning it back off. Refer to *"Turning Airplane Mode On and Off"* on page 134 to learn how to turn Airplane mode off.
- **Area code** - Make sure you dialed an area code with the phone number.
- **Restart** - Turn the phone off and back on, as this sometimes solves the problem.

4. Can't surf the web

Make sure the mobile network or Wi-Fi is turned on. Refer to *"Enabling or Disabling the Data Connection"* on page 135 or refer to *"Setting Up Wi-Fi"* on page 127 to learn more.

5. Screen or keyboard does not rotate

If the screen does not turn or the full, horizontal keyboard is not showing when the phone is turned on its side, the problem may be one of the following issues:

- It is very likely that the application does not support the horizontal view.
- Make sure that the phone is not lying flat while rotating. Hold the phone upright to change the orientation in applications that support it.
- Make sure Auto-Rotate is turned on. Refer to *"Turning Auto-Rotate On or Off"* on page 152 to learn more.

6. Low Microphone Volume, Caller can't hear you

If you are talking to someone who has trouble hearing you, try removing any cases or other accessories, as these may cover up the microphone. If the caller cannot hear you at all, you may have accidentally muted the conversation. To learn how to turn mute on or off while on a call, refer to *"Using the Mute Function During a Voice Call"* on page 30.

If you find yourself accidentally muting the conversation often, there may be something covering up the light sensor, preventing the screen from dimming and locking the mute button. Taking off any accessories may also correct this problem, as some cases cover up the sensor completely.

7. Display does not adjust brightness automatically

If the phone does not dim in dark conditions or does not become brighter in bright conditions, try taking any cases or accessories off. Cases may block the light sensor at the top of the phone, located near the earpiece. Also, Auto Brightness may be turned off. To learn how to turn Auto-Brightness on or off, refer to *"Adjusting the Brightness"* on page 148.

8. Application does not install correctly

Sometimes applications may not download or install correctly. If this happens, try canceling the download and re-downloading the application. If the application is already installed, try uninstalling an application and re-installing it. Refer to *"Uninstalling an Application"* on page 118 to learn more.

9. Touchscreen does not respond as expected

If there is a problem with the touchscreen, try the following, in the order in which the steps appear:

1. Remove any cases or screen protectors from the touchscreen.
2. Clean the screen with a soft, damp cloth.
3. Wash and dry your hands thoroughly. Grease and other residue on your skin may cause the touchscreen to function improperly.
4. Restart your device to clear any temporary software bugs.

10. Phone becomes very hot

Some applications require a lot of power and may cause the phone to become hot to the touch. This is normal and should not affect your device's life span or performance.

11. Camera does not turn on

If the camera does not turn on, try one of the following:

- Make sure the phone's battery is fully charged.
- Free up some memory by transferring files to a PC or deleting files from your device, as there may not be enough remaining memory to store new pictures. Refer to *"Freeing Up Memory"* on page 176 to learn more.
- Restart the phone and try turning on the camera again.

Index

Other Books from the Author of the Help Me Series, Charles Hughes

Help Me! Guide to the iPhone 5S

Help Me! Guide to the Nexus 7

Help Me! Guide to the Galaxy S4

Help Me! Guide to the Kindle Fire HDX

Help Me! Guide to the HTC One

Help Me! Guide to the iPhone 4

Help Me! Guide to the iPod Touch

Help Me! Guide to the iPad Mini

Help Me! Guide to the Kindle Touch

Help Me! Guide to the Samsumg Galaxy Note

Help Me! Guide to the iPad Air